# Renegades

**ISBN2** 979-8-3993902-0-8

**Captured, Curated, and Articulated** McKenzie Reeves Decker
**Proofreader** Hannah Vincent and Keith Wasserstrom
**Front Cover** Jen Odom
**Book Designer** Jen Odom

Printed and bound in the United States of America.

To learn more, visit systemandsoul.com

# BENJ MILLER

### with Chris White and McKenzie Decker

# ENDORSEMENTS

[your glowing endorsement here]

# ACKNOWLEDGEMENTS

Our Father in Heaven who created us,
loves us, and seeks union with us.

Jesus who paid the price for union with Father.

The Holy Spirit who guides and counsels us.

Our spouses who champion us and refine us.
Erica Miller
Darlene White
Jake Decker

Our mentors, advisors, coaches, and peers for their
necessary community and encouragement.
John Richie
Tim Spiker
Robby Angle
John Ott
Clark and Kim Miller
Venture and the Wolfpack
Atlanta Operator Forum
Lt. Col Scott Mann
Dino Signore Ph.d.
Jonathan B. Smith

Our System & Soul staff, coaches, and Renegade-
contributors that made this book possible.

# TABLE OF CONTENTS

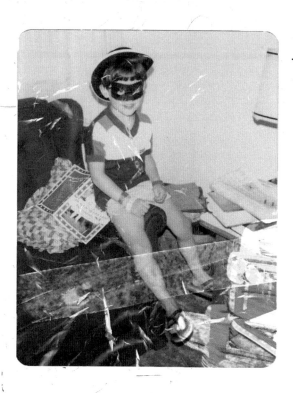

*"Entrepreneurship is the last refuge
of the troublemaking individual."*
– Natalie Clifford Barney

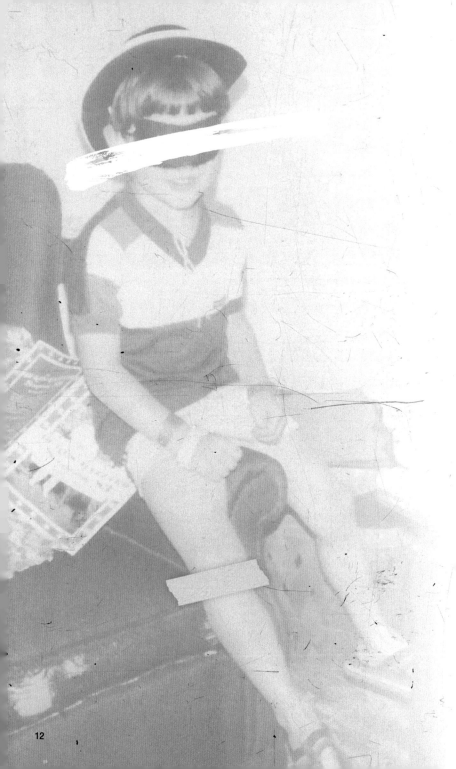

# PREFACE

Hi, I'm benj.

This is me in 2003. At the time I'm writing this book—20 years later—I've gotten rid of the frosted tips and earrings. Although, you never know when that look might make a comeback.

I've also become a completely different version of that guy in more ways than one.

That guy was pretty impatient to get where he wanted to go. He had lightning-bolt ideas and ran at everything full speed. He thought he knew a lot about a lot. He liked being different. He liked being busy, and maybe a little overwhelmed. He loved risks and pushing the envelope.

He was a Renegade if there ever was one:

- Telling my elementary math teacher he **knew**
  a better way to solve the problem

- Inventing a 30,000 sq. ft. youth hangout facility

- Designing his own clothes

- Grinding while everyone else was
  "YOLO-ING" through high-school

So, maybe you'd expect me to say a lot of those things have
changed. They haven't. What I would say is, I think I've upgraded/
evolved. Still a Renegade, just under new motivations.

I think the best and worst of me have often been two sides
of the same coin—one side driven by fear of losing, missing
out, failing, or being mediocre, and the other side driven
by love, gratitude, and a greater sense of true identity.

In my journey, I've been a part of starting 10 businesses.
Some of my businesses are thriving, and others just didn't
make the cut. One company started as just me and a laptop
designing logos for local brands. 20-years later that business
employs dozens of talented marketers and helped some of
the world's best-known brands. Three of my businesses have
sold. And one, I'd call my biggest failure, included renovating
a tour bus that ended in flames (literally and figuratively).

In every case, regardless of success or failure, the Renegade
in me would eventually be tested. The business sometimes
desperately needed me to innovate or break us out of a
funk, and then at other times, seemed to spend excess
time fixing what I messed up. I learned over time to
recognize these tensions as they happened, and it shapes
when and how I show up in my companies today.

But that awareness and shift in my thinking didn't happen overnight, or even in a short season of time. It didn't happen because I launched successful businesses or knew a lot of other successful people. It happened so much slower than the 2003 Benj would be able to handle. It happened because I learned what I truly wanted out of my life and work—freedom to be myself, be the best version of the person I was made to be, and give everyone else in my life the dignity to do the same.

Some of the change in me happened on purpose, and some of it happened despite me. A lot of it happened because I eventually started listening to the people willing to give me honest feedback: John Richie, Erica Miller, Chris White, Mckenzie Decker, Jason Ogden... the list goes on. Maybe 100s of people over time who have shown me how to shift the lens to my kaleidoscope and see something entirely new.

Several years ago, I stepped out of running the businesses I'd founded/co-founded and started coaching business owners on all the ways I'd learned to shift my thinking for the better.

Let's just say, it didn't go well right out of the gate.

One of my first clients was a founder who wanted me to come in and help her figure out how to accelerate growth and hold her team accountable, but she was stuck in being the Chief Everything Officer. What I could see right away was that she needed to stop driving every project, conversation, and decision in the business.

She was standing over every shoulder in her 100-person company and everyone was afraid to do their job without first getting her approval. Consequently, they couldn't quite figure out who was responsible for what exactly. Tasks and responsibilities seemed to get delegated more often to whoever happened to be walking by her office than to the right person in the right role. She was exhausted. The team was confused. And they weren't getting anywhere near their future revenue and profit projections.

She needed to give her people a chance to step up and demonstrate their ability. She needed to delegate 90% of what she was doing, spend more time training her top performers, and scheduled a long vacation so they could prove to her that they were capable of running the show. So, that's what I told her.

She didn't like my advice, and at first, I couldn't figure out her resistance. I'd just given her the golden ticket to bypass 20 more years of learning things the hard way and the freedom to go live her life without being everything to everyone. In meeting with her and other founders like her over the years, I discovered that while I knew I'd learned a lot of helpful ways to eliminate problems in their business, I was missing the biggest challenge of all.

When my client said she wanted to accelerate and she wanted accountability, she meant, "I want to fix this business. I need help, but I don't want to lose my value in it. I have so much to offer this business. I've literally carried it on my back up until now. It's part of me and I care more than anyone here that we see it succeed. Don't count me out. Don't make me irrelevant."

DUH, Benj. Of course. Who would hand over what they've invested decades of time into just because one guy with a binder full of mental models and team exercises says it's the best move?

And even more so, what Renegade gives in so easily without first putting up a fight?

Once I realized that the founders I was working with were fighting the same fight I had fought over and over since those frosted tips days, I realized that I couldn't just give them a manual to do things how I had done them.

They didn't operate that way, and if I wanted to truly help them, I had to remember to champion their dignity above all, and prescribing something out of the box wasn't what dignity looked like.

Dignity was helping them discover on their own how their genius—breaking the right rules, ignoring the noise that everyone else gets distracted by, following their gut—had a perfect place in their future business. I was one of 100s of voices telling them the right next step, but if I wanted them to see the path, they needed to know I was fighting alongside them.

O: The

# Dilemma

Chapter 0

# THE DILEMMA

I never set out to write a business book.
Seriously. Who needs *another* business book?
And yet… here we are.
Not because I became an overnight expert.
Not because I was suddenly struck with inspiration.
Not because my ego got the best of me.

Here's what changed my mind:

The book I needed, I couldn't find anywhere…

The book that helped me do a tough, lonely job…

The book about how to **keep your freedom
as an entrepreneur and not get stuck in
the grind of a growing business.**

When I started coaching founders, and I saw I wasn't the only
one who needed a better way, that's what changed my mind.

As a founder, you are the only one who cares about the future of the business, the product, the ideas, all the revenue streams, relationships, and clients for a long time, years maybe. Most of us start out without a capable team so we had to do all the *stuff*. And for a while, that works... until it doesn't.

Overtime, if we run the business well enough, we end up needing to build a team to help pave the way forward. But when that happens, suddenly we have more cats to herd and problems to solve than ever before. Worst of all, the energy and focus we need to really do our jobs—the job of the leader charting the course, bettering the product, or unlocking the market—gets swallowed whole by day-to-day chaos.

As I've faced this challenge over the years, I've learned a few ways to get beyond the chaos. Looking back, I think entrepreneurs like us need a resource that helps us have the freedom to keep building and dreaming about our business that doesn't require every aspect to orbit around us when it should leverage the best of us.

I always felt like the freedom I had when I started a business was just out of reach as the business grew, and I struggled to get it back. I felt like my options were to give up trying to get that freedom back, or give up the business so I could have my freedom.

In the decades I've spent building and coaching businesses, I've continually run into the mess so many of us face when we go from lone ranger to suddenly herding a stampede.

If you're like me, you've read all of the classic business books to find the solution.

We gain a little freedom when our businesses have better systems, so we've read about systems. We enforce structure, hierarchy, and the rules we play by.

There is so much wisdom to gain from the business gurus who told us how great businesses are run—

| | |
|---|---|
| *The Advantage* | by Patrick Lencioni |
| *The E–Myth* | by Michael Gerber |
| *Good to Great* | by Jim Collins |
| *Principles* | by Ray Dalio |
| *Rockefeller Habits* | by Verne Harnish |
| *Traction* | by Gino Wickman |
| *The 4-Hour Work Week* | by Tim Ferriss |
| *Measure what Matters* | by John E. Doerr |

and so many more.

The systematic thinking of these leaders changed the way so many of us run the day-to-day of our organizations.

But the business feels dead inside if it's all about following rules and meeting protocols. We recognize that we didn't just need systems, we needed "soul" to make the business come alive—culture, purpose, leadership to make what we're doing matter.

So we've all read books about that, too.

*How to Win Friends
and Influence People*     by Dale Carnegie

*The 7 Habits of Highly
Effective People*     by Stephen Covey

*5 Dysfunctions
of a Team*     by Patrick Lencioni

*Dare to Lead*     by Brene Brown

*Start with Why*     by Simon Sinek

*The Culture Code*     by Daniel Coyle

and so many more.

All of these books are wonderful and incredibly helpful. I'd even say they're necessary. They reshape the way we interact and lead in our work. Frankly though, they all just left me with more to do. I wasn't feeling like I had regained my sense of freedom. I was still head-down trying to keep the wheels from falling off.

I was left asking:

How do I actually do ALL of this and get the real me back?

How does it all fit together in a way that doesn't compound my work?

I needed someone to release the pressure valve, not add more to my to-do list.

There was also another tension to contend
with inside the business itself:

If I systematized everything, we'd build a rigid box
around everything inventive we'd created. That didn't
feel right. My business would become just another
soulless machine making average widgets.

And if I wanted to instill a real soul in our business, I knew it
would be messy, hard to carry out, and maybe even useless. Soul
seems elusive, soft, and hard to quantify. Worst of all… what if
I failed? What if nobody "got it" or it didn't make a difference?

Then I realized I had a much bigger challenge in
front of me than the one I was trying to solve. It
had nothing to do with anything I'd read.

**My dilemma was this:**

**1.** I don't like systems. I don't like rules. I don't want
to be confined or restricted. I am a Renegade!
Systems would kill the very nature of me.

**2.** I was stuck trying to make the best choices for the
business. I felt like I had to choose one and lose the
other: the systems or the soul. The business needed
systems. It needed boundaries. It needed more clarity
about the direction we were going than to follow my
current whim. It needed to have some control.

**3.** I desperately needed to regain the freedom to
be the Renegade, visionary, founder, inventor,
and dreamer while my business scaled.

**This was the problem I needed to solve.**

If that tension and deeply-held desire feels relatable, welcome to the club.

*You are a Renegade.*

I'm glad you're here.

If you're working with (or surviving) a Renegade, I'm glad you're here as well. This book will help you understand this seemingly untameable human being and partner with them. And maybe, just maybe, it will awaken a little Renegade within yourself.

I wrote this book for us to find a way to have our freedom without sacrificing any of what we've built. To lead as Renegades— free to imagine, focus on the future, and chase possibilities, while building a healthy, stable, mature business to scale.

This book is for those of us who are ready to cross the gap from being the Renegade-Founder to being the Renegade-Leader of an audacious team, one that will move beyond anything you could build on your own.

I've found that freedom comes to us when we let go and invite in a team of capable leaders to help us take our dream to scale. But let's be clear—we're not going to play by the rules as they're set. Again—not how I roll—and not how you do either. Let's reimagine what it looks like to get ahead, build the business you dream of faster, more efficiently, and holistically *without* trading your soul.

Welcome to the *third option, Renegades.*

Before we dive in, I have to warn you, this new way of thinking about your business isn't for everyone.

Don't read this book if...

- You want to remain oblivious to the problems you're causing.

- You're unwilling to face your fears.

- You refuse to lean into your own vulnerability.

Because the third option is as much about looking inward at yourself as it is about evaluating your business.

Your ability to own up, grow up, let go, be vulnerable, and move forward with courage is everything.

**Let's**

# 2: The

SKEPTICS.

# REBELS

RULE BREAKERS.

Chapter 1

# THE RENEGADE

**What is a renegade?**
ren·e·gade
/ˈren ə gād/

A person who deserts a set of principles.

*skeptic. rebel. rule breaker.*

You know them when you see them.

| | |
|---|---|
| Peter Pan | Rob Dydrek |
| Katniss Everdeen | Elvis |
| William Wallace | Mark Cuban |
| Tommy Boy | Mike Tyson |
| Russell Simmons | Ferris Buller |
| Elon Musk | MacGuyver |
| Sarah Blakely | *(the original, not the reboot)* |
| Neo | Mr. Keating |

(We'll explain some of these examples later.)

They are the individuals who defy stereotypes, refuse to check boxes, stand in line, or follow the process. They're partly driven by their rebel spirit and partly by curiosity. The quiet misfits. The tinkerers. The one with the summer job in high school employing other kids to cut lawns for them. The kid who'd lend you lunch money but with 10% interest. Smart. Different. Hard to peg in any one category and proud of their individuality.

They're the people who look past the options laid out in front of them, and by some magic feat, see a crazy vision of what could be, then figure out how to get there.

- Apps that let you share your life in pictures.

- Watches that can serve as a life-alert, home security system, sleep monitor, and phone.

- Online marketplaces that deliver for free, with same-day shipping.

- Pharmacies that make the cost of most medicines less than a cup of coffee.

- Ice cream flavors designed purely on smell instead of taste.

- Computer systems that can write, draw, think, translate, and create for you.

They speak their own language and are often saying,

"What if…"

"I have an idea…"

"Let's try this instead…"

"I bet I can do it better."

"How could we…"

Sometimes their instincts lead them to revelations and breakthroughs that change the way the world works. And then other times, they start fires that burn perfectly good work to the ground (more to come on that).

Renegades are uniquely gifted at the starting line, bolting forward with a new idea, and initiating it before anyone else can leave the starting block.

Renegades are well-loved for their "genius" and "out of the box" thinking. Their willingness to not fit in is intriguing and magnetic. They are usually self-appointed leaders—people who don't have time or patience for raises and promotions doled out by someone else. They are very often natural-born entrepreneurs or disgruntled employees who believe they can do it all better than the boss (and they are probably right).

If you are the Renegade, you get it. You have the ability to see more than what's in front of you and you're built to chase down possibility. But for all of our profound abilities and unique insights, our grand ideas, and extreme optimism doesn't always guarantee success.

Harvard Business School Professor William Sahlman says, "For every Amazon or Uber, there are scores of companies few can remember." You really don't need a Harvard professor to tell you that, but now you have. As Renegades, we live this reality all the time. So, what separates successful Renegades from those that fail and don't recover? Ask the professor. Sahlman also says, "When a company succeeds, it's because it has discovered and made the right moves along the way."

We'll spend a lot of time in this book unpacking HOW to make the right moves and channel that Renegade energy into freedom for you, and success for your business.

**The amazing**—often unexpected— insight is that your freedom and your business' success are **highly correlated.**

**Here's the deal:**

You got this far because you're really good at breaking rules when they are worth breaking.

You're also really good at finding a better way and going hard after it.

But, if that was working perfectly, you wouldn't be reading this book.

You're building something amazing.

You see something that could be better, faster, smarter, cheaper, and you're making it happen.

You're doing the daily work to bring it to life.

You're catalyzing change in an industry that no one else could make possible.

You're creating jobs and ensuring the livelihood of other people in your community.

You're altering the social landscape of your community forever.

You're changing the course of your family tree for generations.

You're designing your own life.

You should feel like you're on top of the world.

But you're stuck in the business. It's swallowing you whole and it sucks. This wasn't part of the vision you had in mind.

*"The walls of self-protection you build around yourself become walls of self-imprisonment over a period of time."* —Sadhguru

If we can be honest though,

*most of us have built our **own prisons**.*

We work twice as hard. Have twice as much stress. Carry all the responsibility. And sometimes earn half the pay to stay a Renegade.

I've known Renegades who have taken meetings and closed business deals while they're in labor at the hospital. I've known Renegades who answered emails on their wedding day. I've known Renegades who spent years traveling 3+ days a week to speak at conferences without getting paid just to get established. And I've been the Renegade who sacrificed health, regular exercise, time really getting to be with my kids, and sleep for the sake of the business.

It doesn't work without our fire.
And it also seems, no matter how hard we work for our business; it doesn't work for us.

Too often, Renegades **end up** prioritizing their business and let so many other areas **of life suffer. And** worse, it's easy to justify.

*Work* **feels like 96% with 1% left for**
**Hobbies** *"My work is my hobby."*
**Health** *"I'll have more time to focus on myself when..."*
**Relationships** *"They understand."*
**Family** *"I'm doing this for them."*
**Work** *"It needs me or else..."*

I want to show you how I've not only gotten to the other side of the mess as a Renegade, but also how these ideas have helped thousands of other business owners do the same.

Some have quadrupled revenue and maximized profits. Some have turned a crappy culture into a recognized "Best Place to Work." Some went from 10 employees to 300 employees. Some have sold their businesses for a 15X multiple. Some have been able to retire and empower a team of leaders that they are confident can take things forward. And ALL OF THEM would tell you they feel freedom in a way they felt like they lost a long time ago.

**Here's the gist. We've got a short list to tackle, but it's going to be challenging.**

**1.** We gotta talk about the shit show you're in and why it's happening. Face reality.

**2.** Then, we need to lay the foundation for how you get out of it. Do the groundwork.

**3.** Next, you've got some important decisions to make. Shift your thinking.

**4.** Lastly, there's a plot twist, but it's all good news.

Note: As a Renegade, I KNOW you hate labels and narrowly defined boxes, so take the experiences and recommendations in this book for what you will. Not everything here applies to every founder's story, but I think you'll find a few ideas that ring true for you and can help you get to the other side of the gap.

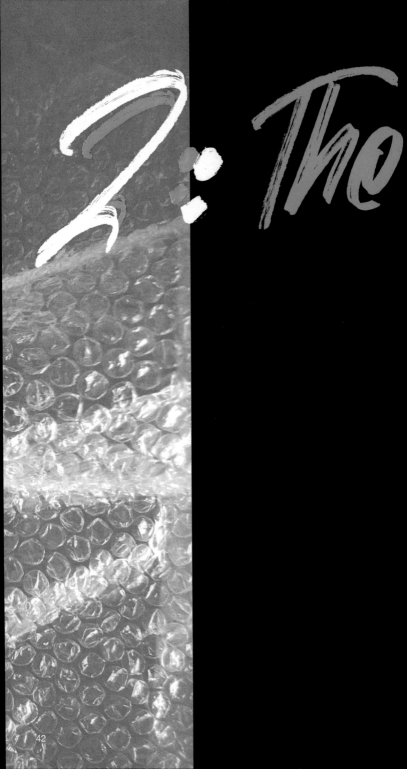

2: The

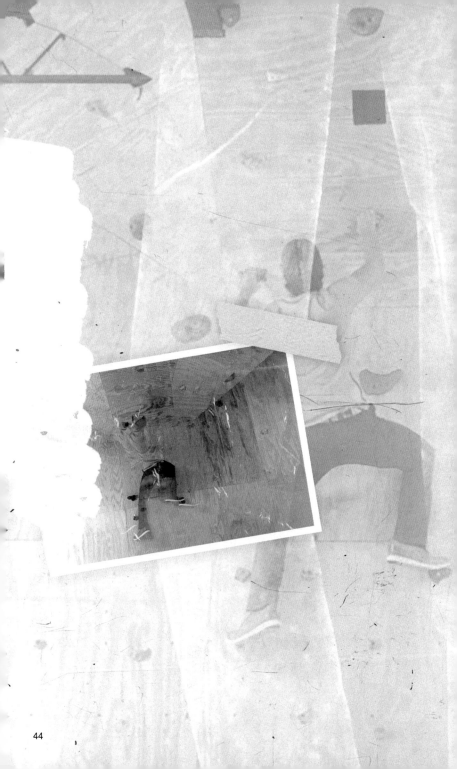

Chapter 2

# THE SHIT SHOW

For the first five years of running my marketing agency, there were a lot of moments for my Renegade-thinking to shine.

I built a network that helped us close some huge, high-profile deals before we ever had a well-known reputation for our work.

I pivoted projects when inspiration struck, and we delivered insanely innovative solutions for our clients.

I even designed our office space to include a rock climbing wall and a foosball table (before it was cliche)—to make my business an inviting, unique place to work.

I didn't feel like we had major issues holding us back as a business or stunting our growth, but I took the advice of a friend, who recommended that even if it looked good from my seat, I should have a consultant come in to evaluate the business. If you'd asked me then, I was 100% certain we had a healthy, happy team and a pretty great business. I knew we would ace this consultant's evaluation. It was basically going to be a waste of time.

Yet, within the first half hour of our consultation, I realized the business I thought I'd built was not the one everyone else experienced.

Where I thought we were fun and flexible—loose titles, even looser meetings, and the freedom to create without much direction—my team voiced that the way we operated was chaotic.

Where I thought I was taking mediocre work to the next level when I swooped in and changed the designs we would deliver to the client the day before a presentation, my team was frustrated by a lack of process and feeling sidelined.

Where I thought my rock climbing wall and foosball table was creating a cool culture, they were just wishing they had clearer job descriptions.

I thought what I'd built was pretty good. And in a way it was... but it wasn't working for everyone. In those days, more people's opinions were beginning to matter than when I was going solo. Challenges I'd never considered surfaced that day sitting in that room with my team. I realized then what all Renegades have to face eventually:

**My Renegade-Founder thinking was not the only fuel we needed anymore to take us where we needed to go.**

I became aware that day, but it took me a long time to understand and accept.

The truth is—no matter how hard we fight and push back and cleverly out-think the change we face—being a Renegade seemingly comes to a screeching halt as soon as the business needs more than invention, ideas, and drive.

Practically speaking, that usually looks like when the business reaches 15-25 employees, or when it passes the 7-figure mark, but it can vary for everyone. Some call it reaching a "Control Stage" or "Stage 2." All of this is dependent on several factors, but it looks the same in every case:

Find product-market fit.

Demand grows.

Revenue increases enough to hire more people.

Promote a few people into leadership roles.

People start asking for processes.

~~Maybe~~ you become a bottleneck.

When you change your mind, people get frustrated.

When you don't follow the process, people get frustrated.

When you wing it, go off script, do it your way, or call an audible, people get frustrated.

You don't get what the big deal is, and you start to feel like an enemy in your own camp.

Maybe you even keep decisions from them until you absolutely have to tell them.

**For the Renegade-Founder, being a Renegade at this stage can feel like constantly stepping on *landmines* in a place you used to *run* free.**

You start to internalize that the team "just doesn't get it."

For the team working with a Renegade, it can feel like you've become an arsonist.

Where they once lit a fire within the team, motivating, inspiring and helping them see what's not yet there, the fire gets out of hand and creeps into everything good that's been built.

The rule-breaking Renegade starts to break down
the effectiveness and unity of the organization.

Running into the mess becomes running non-stop.

Betting on themselves and changing the
cards becomes chronic whiplash.

Figuring it out as they go becomes inconsistent
delivery and chaotic systems.

Seizing the day becomes burnout.

Being whoever they want to be becomes an identity crisis.

Making their own way becomes
leaving the team in the dust.

Left unchecked, the Renegade-Arsonist ends up driving the
business into misalignment, discourages their best talent from
sticking around to extinguish the flames, and ultimately creates
a problem only they can solve—putting down the matches.

It's not that easy though.
TWO SIDES, SAME STORY.

# TWO SIDES,

## Renegade Feeling

I have more at stake than anyone.

This is my business. Of course I want it to be successful. They need the way I think and my intuition, otherwise we'd be dead in the water. If we're not constantly inventing and being willing to seize opportunity, we'll stall out.

They just need to be flexible and know that we're the kind of company that moves fast and works hard.

I wish they could just speed up and see where we're trying to go.

# SAME STORY

## Team Thinking

He has no idea what it takes to pull this off and how much harder and more complicated he makes it every time he changes course.

We should just hold out and wait to take action on anything knowing he's just going to come in tomorrow and change his mind.

It's hard to feel like we're winning. And it's even harder as a manager to explain to my team how this constant change is tied to our vision and goals (I'm not even sure…).

I wish he could just slow down long enough to see what he's doing.

## THE THIRD OPTION

As business coaches we hear both sides—kind of like doing couples therapy. Before I go on, I want you to hear from someone who sees the other side of this problem as she both survives and supports the Renegade in me. McKenzie Decker is my Operator and business partner at System & Soul. She, like a lot of the people on your leadership team and in your organization, has felt the tension we're talking about. She likes having a plan, setting a path and sticking to it. She is risk-averse, suspicious of sudden change, and wants to do things the "right way." I know I drive her crazy.

If you don't already know, you drive people like her crazy. But, I also know she is my biggest fan and the constant protector of my dream for the business we're building.

I want you to know her perspective because at times, I think you and I don't champion the dignity of our best allies (our team) much less our own dignity in the process of getting to the dream. But when we lean in and listen, we might find a pathway to dignity for all.

## TAKE IT FROM A RENEGADE:

*McKenzie Reeves Decker*

Operator/COO and Co-Founder of System & Soul

*First and foremost, I think it's so important to keep in mind, the feelings on both sides are mutual, and for good reason. Our Renegades feel trapped in an endless loop and so do our teams. The problem is, we tend to stay stuck when we're only interested in our side of the story and getting it resolved how we see fit.*

*Over the years as I've worked on teams and served as a leader, I've watched the same disappointing patterns play out over and over again between Renegades and their teams as they seek out one-sided solutions.*

### HIDING

*The Renegade stops communicating with the team about decisions, deals, and ideas and finds new ways to excite their own interest and engage opportunities.*

*The Team hides—perhaps literally—whenever the Renegade is in the office and trying to round up everyone for an impromptu brainstorm session. They hide their plans and quietly push their own agendas forward hoping to go unnoticed.*

*Ultimately, what results is division, secrecy, and a growing lack of trust on both sides.*

## DISENGAGEMENT

*The Renegade gets bored and assumes the spark in the business is dead. Maybe it's time to sell. Maybe it's time to start a new venture. Their mind drifts to far off places and more interesting prospects while their team scrambles to deal with the problems of today.*

*The team gets discouraged to the point of wondering if it's worth it. Why work this hard when the Renegade is only going to change their mind? Lots of great talent finds its way out of environments like this that feel underappreciated or ineffective for the work they feel equipped to do.*

## DEFENSE

*The Renegade, being on their island, making their own way, starts to resent their team and begins guarding what they've built, fearing it's all at risk of being ruined by the lack-luster approach everyone else takes. Maybe worse, the Renegade starts to fear the future for themselves, wondering if it will always be this confining. The fear of losing their personal freedom grows.*

*The team withholds their creative thinking. They think, why would I give up my good ideas to someone who doesn't want to share the stage? They collude and form a firm, withdrawn defense against the Renegade who they see as equally out of touch with what's really happening on the ground floor of the business, and how her visionary ideas turn into more distractions for them to manage.*

From my experience, the real challenge here is not to determine who is right or wrong or who will eventually give in. It's so much more about being able to see and appreciate the very real perspective coming from both sides. The Renegade sees their world in terms of quickly passing moments of opportunity. The team thrives on clarity and having the time and space to do their best work.

If, let's say, our aim at the end of the day is to be a company that champions the dignity of every person who walks through the doors, our challenge, I believe, is to be able to find common ground and common purpose in the fact that we all want the same outcome—to win in our work, and know that what we contribute matters. We need our Renegades to help drive us forward. We need the team to build the bridge and pave the road in the right direction. But I don't think this just happens because we compromise or agree to disagree.

One of the most important things that wild-Renegade Benj has demonstrated to me and the teams he leads is that really being able to solve this problem inside our organizations starts with the problem within us as individuals.

# 2.5: The
## with the

Chapter 2.5

# THE PROBLEM WITH THE PROBLEM

Here's the problem you already know you have…

YOU CAN'T KEEP THIS UP.

I mean, you can, but I doubt you want to live
another 20 or 30 year by the mantra:

25 hours a day, 7 days a week, hustle, grind, repeat.
My ideas
My time
My input
Me
Myself
I

As a coach, I meet with founders all the time to talk about
the challenges they face when they grow the business
to a point that no longer works the way it used to.

Often, it seems to them like they lost their magic.

"We can't find the right people and get them to stay."
"We've been stuck for three years and
our profitability hasn't budged."
"We can't keep up with what our customers need
from us. Our reputation is in jeopardy."
"We are losing out to our competitors and we don't know why."

I've worked with one Renegade-Founder, Jason Moore, who
started a healthcare technology company in 2010. When we
started working together, he was completely stuck. He'd spent
a decade building his business, and he'd done pretty well. They
had a team of 10 people running a 5-million-dollar operation
and market conditions were great for the foreseeable future.

They plotted out a decent amount of growth for
the next few years, but nothing epic.
Quietly, he was pretty disenchanted with the whole
business (as any true Renegade would be). Overtime,
he wasn't thrilled with the results, and definitely wasn't
motivated by marginal, status quo progress. Even more
so, he wasn't proud of the culture they'd built.

The leaders he'd promoted to help him were more of a drag
on the future than a catalyst. It wasn't like he was sitting on his
hands either. He'd read all the business books you're supposed
to read. He made his team read those books too. But nothing
changed. As the slog continued, he met with his board of
investors. They were unhappy with the company's projections
and challenged him to find a new way forward. But he was
stuck. He just couldn't figure out how to do it differently.

Underneath the conversation we're having about the
business' languishing bottomline, there was a story
unfolding that founders like him are often afraid to admit.

*He* couldn't figure out how to do it *his way.* His sheer will, drive and abilities—they'd been game-changing before. Hell, the business survived on it for 5 full years—but it wasn't enough anymore. And he was exhausted.

**Welcome To The shit show.**

This common story takes on many voices for Renegade-Founders at this point:

**The Frustrated Critic:** "I've done everything right, and now I feel imprisoned by my own creation."

**The Doomed Free Spirit:** "I'm becoming a slave to this business. "I'm losing sleep and the freedom I thought I'd have by starting my own thing."

**The Anxious Controller:** "I'm still the one that has to fix everything."

**The Agitated Achiever:** "Without me this business would have no drive. It would die. "I'm still spending tons of time making sure people are actually doing what they are supposed to."

**The Martyr:** "Why don't they care as much as I do?"

**The Jaded Inventor:** "I wanted to build something different, nuanced, something people would crave, something amazing and it's just so… average.

They are all thinking, "I built this so I could own it, not let it run my life. I want freedom and I want this to work. But I don't know how to have both."

# Renegade-Founder

Founder's

# Renegade-Leader

## Gap

**This is the Founder's Gap.**

It's the seemingly bottomless, impossible to traverse, sure to suck you in, and ultimately deadly gap to cross from the business you built to the business you want to own.

The Gap might be visible in the business itself— flatlined growth, rising or consistently high turnover, or a culture of confusion, apathy, or reactivity.

Sometimes though, the symptoms don't readily show themselves in the business or balance sheet. Not on the surface anyway.

More often the Gap starts internally with you, the Founder. And either you suffer silently or slowly start to leak out into your organization. But it always flows from you.

**The Founder's Gap exists for a few distinct reasons:**

1. **Personal**: as a founder you'll always struggle to see your business without distortion. You'll have a tendency to see it as much better, or much worse than it is.

2. **Structural**: the systems and behaviors you've created in the business (accidental or intentional) don't support what you'll need to function at scale.

3. **Philosophical**: and this fixes the first two reasons if you can figure it out. **The Gap exists because of how you see yourself as the Renegade-Founder and how you create value in the world.**

Circle one. Or two. Or all three.

Renegades, we all get here. This is our journey. And you should know that what you want is not wrong. It's not unattainable. It's not complicated. It's just so damn hard. It's particularly hard for you because you have to face your own identity in the business.

If who you are is what you do, how you perform, and what you can accomplish, then you're leaving a lot up to chance, to the full range of your emotions, and to outside circumstances. And where you go… your business follows.

My coach and mentor, John Richie, brilliantly articulates, "The root of all business issues flow from the *heart* of the leader."

The business follows the heart you bring into it. If you're jaded, resentful, afraid, angry, insecure, or apathetic, then your business will be right on your heels. We can't deny the fact that we are central to the health and growth of the entity we created. It doesn't stand apart from us, and it's reactive to whatever version of ourselves we bring to it.

- If our identity is rooted in our success, and we're not achieving the success we feel we need…

- If our identity is rooted in being the smartest, or being "ahead of the curve" and we make mistakes or we don't have the answers anymore…

- If our identity is rooted in being independent, being able to do it all on your own, and you're running out of capacity, or reaching a ceiling for what you can truly handle…

**The business will react.**

Every decision we make is laced with this urgency and panic
to fill the void, protect the ego, and restore the identity.

It probably feels unfair and maybe unhealthy to be this integrated
into the life of our businesses. But it also feels like your role right
now is far too incumbent on the direction of the business.

What we need to do is recognize the power we hold,
examine the identity that is impacting the business, and then
work to create a healthy separation between the two.

Make no mistake, who you are as you lead and what's at the
heart of you will always have an impact on this business. I
want to equip you to stand more resilient, steady, and aligned
to your vision so the business can leverage the best of you.

My own version of misplaced identity caused one of the biggest
business mistakes and personal failures I've ever known.

About 12 years ago, I refused help from a leader and it ended up
costing me more than half of my business seemingly overnight.

At that point, my marketing business was in a stable and rapid
growth phase. I was known in my community as a successful
founder and a gifted strategist. I felt like I was deep in my skill
set and winning big. So, when this leader tried to give me crucial
feedback and offered to partner with me in my business, I just
didn't have a whole lot of room for his offer or investment.

Back then, all I could think was….

- He was trying to take this business I'd built.

- He didn't understand it like I did.

- I didn't want to lose my freedom.

We don't take the entrepreneurial leap just to have someone step in and turn our thing into another watered-down, overly-democratic, out-of-the-box business.

I certainly hadn't.

At the time, I would have told you whole-heartedly that I was protecting an asset. I had 100 reasons why this guy was wrong and 200 reasons why *I* was right. On paper or in a court of law, I would have been convincing.

The problem, as I look back on it, wasn't with the advice I was given. It wasn't about him or his proposal. It wasn't really even about the business and protecting this amazing place I'd spent so much time in.

**It was really about me.** My business and its success was *everything.* Without really being conscious of it, I was living and dying each day by what the business said about me. If the business was successful, I was successful. If it was chaotic, I would feel incredibly anxious. If someone else was leading in it, then what would I do? I needed the business because it made me valuable.

So, when I turned down his offer, the business took a plunge. It lost its value, and so did I.

I can't say I've ever been at a lower point in my life. I'd completely lost my sense of identity.

To have your identity stripped away is a painful, shocking, and empty feeling. I was contending with what this failure said about me as a person while I tried to salvage any pieces of the business that were left. I had no energy or confidence to do what I needed to do to move forward. I was confused, afraid, and felt so insignificant. There was not enough I could DO anymore to create value.

I went back to counting our cash in terms of weeks remaining until we ran out of money and lay awake at night rehearsing how I would tell the amazing team I hired that they would need to start looking for other jobs. I felt like I was captaining a sinking ship, but at the same time I was scrambling to find a way to salvage it, calling friends and emailing clients for more work opportunities as fast as I could. Underlying the work I was doing nonstop, I was fighting this overwhelming shame and defeat. All I wanted to do was hit stop on this nightmare and walk away.

This was the very bottom of my Founder's Gap. And I was the one to blame, but not for the reasons I believed at the time. In the midst of that low—it took a while for me to see the truth about myself.

You may not have experienced a failure that set you back after years of work. Not everyone does. But what's necessary for us to understand and take to heart is that moving from Renegade-Founder to Renegade-Leader is first a personal decision, then an organizational one.

GO AHEAD
I'LL WAIT

You have to decide what well you want to draw water out of. If your identity is rooted in all that you can accomplish and how powerful a force you can be, you will quickly run dry.

If your identity is rooted deep in who you are, you never run out of resources to give. We never worry that we'll be empty, useless, or without value.

In the next section I want to give you six choices I had to make to escape the Founder's Gap and take my organizations to scale.

If you're really challenged by this problem of the Renegade identity issue, I want to give you a few questions to reflect on before you jump ahead. Take some time to think through these; really be honest with yourself. The more you can know about yourself, the more you'll be able to lead this business to a new level. (Don't judge your answers.)

- What do I want? (really)

- Why do I want what I want?

- What makes me valuable?

- What would other people say makes me valuable?

- What happens if this isn't true anymore or can't be achieved?

- How have I forced this business to support my identity?

*Go ahead. I will wait.*

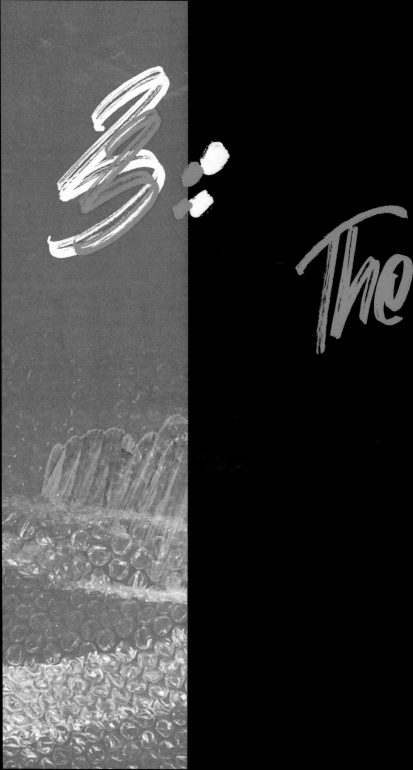

Chapter 3

# THE GROUNDWORK

*"You never change things by fighting the existing reality. To change something, build a new model that makes the existing model obsolete."*
—Inventor and architect, Buckminster Fuller

*Dang, clearly I have some soul searching to do... didn't see that coming.*
*So how do we get out of this so-called Gap?*
*It's dark in here. Anyone bring a flashlight?*

There is a solution to the problems we face through the gap from Renegade-Founder to Renegade-Leader. And like any good story, there are three important obstacles to overcome before we can reach the other side of the mess we're in.

**1.** Your personal sh*t

**2.** Your crew

**3.** The six essential shifts

# Chapter 5

# THE GROUNDWORK

## YOUR PERSONAL SH\*T (IDENTITY)

We will always be pulling back the layers of our identity.
That's part of the journey of being human, and it's a
requirement to becoming an exceptional Renegade-
Leader. If we intend to make genuine, lasting change
that helps our businesses grow, we must start here.

But like I said, I didn't figure it all out after that massive
fallout in my business. I spent a while stumbling around in
the dark before I really understood why my identity mattered
and why it was foundational to be the type of leader I
wanted to be for the type of business I wanted to run.

Here's what I knew…

> I really wanted to be a great leader.
> I wanted to do great work.
> I wanted to provide for my family.
> I wanted to enjoy my life outside of work.

> And… I wanted these outcomes for the people I led, too.

Easy to dream up. Hard to pull off. Especially when success or failure meant that *I* was either a success or failure.

Once I hit that all-time low 15 years ago when my marketing agency plummeted from its stable, respected place in the industry, I realized that it didn't matter if I was the best strategist, or most compelling visionary because I was shaken to the core when strategies didn't go as planned and I couldn't fix all of it. I couldn't sleep. I couldn't think clearly. I spent a lot of time replaying my failures, feeling frustrated, shamed, stupid, angry, and ultimately, exhausted. I needed deeper roots.

With the help of my friend and coach, John Ott and his organization, Exceptional Leaders, I was finally able to put words to what I knew I needed. It comes down to just two things any intentional person can master.

John's coaching was based on a study two of his colleagues, Tim Spiker and Vanessa Kiley, performed in 2016. They looked at the behaviors that measured what made the best leaders effective in their organizations.

They studied 20,000 CEO's to determine that
effectiveness could be summed up in 10 attributes:

- Pursue Vision
- Think Strategically
- Marshal Resources
- Drive Culture
- Ensure Execution
- Others Focused
- Cultivate Talent
- Inwardly Sound
- Unleash Motivation
- Communicate Effectively

BUT here's the shocking part…

**They found that 77% of a leader's effectiveness
is made up of only two of these attributes.**

Before you turn the page… which two
would you bet make up the 77%?

Leadership effectiveness has everything
to do with leaders being:

1. *Inwardly Sound*
2. *Others Focused*

The conclusion in a sentence: well-developed people make
more effective leaders. It's who they are, not what they do.

**Inwardly sound...**
- Secure and settled
- Self-aware
- Principled
- Holistically healthy
- Purposeful

*"Inwardly sound leaders not only LOOK
safe, they ARE safe..."* —Tim Spiker

**Others-focused...**
- Attentive
- Curious
- Empathetic
- Humble
- Heart of service

*"Good leaders must first become good
servants."* —Robert Greenleaf

What letter grade would you give yourself
for each of those 10 bullets?

BECAUSE WHAT YOU'VE *built* IS TOO IMPORTANT TO BE *limited by you.*

I think these outcomes are incredibly underrated in Renegade communities. Value is so often placed on being successful drivers, achievers, communicators, and motivators. But that is just 23% of what makes us truly effective.

Remember in the Marvel movie when Thor lost the power to pick up his hammer when his heart and mind weren't in the right place to lead the great country of Asgar? Yeah, we all have our Thor moment.

That's what it's like when we leave the 77% on the table. Let's retire the idea that leadership is what we do. Leadership starts with who we are.

**Because what you've built is too important to be limited by you.** You are a huge part of finding this freedom and scaling your business. And I guarantee that getting intentional about becoming inwardly sound and others focused in your approach will not only result in a healthier, more productive business, but a better version of yourself.

When I refocused my energy on being a grounded and more holistically healthy version of myself, I had so much less to prove and so much more energy to give to whatever came at me.

The problems I was facing in my floundering business didn't go away. I didn't suddenly rebound. It was long, slow, tedious work. It often looked like making micro decisions every day, every interaction, every meeting to shift my focus and drive to showing up inwardly sound and others focused.

But overtime, I could tell that my team was approaching me differently. I had their attention and focus in a way I didn't have before when the business was all about propping up my ego and hitting big numbers.

What mattered most to me changed. Problems that felt make-or-break suddenly didn't have that much power.

- I could have a contentious conversation with a client and not let it rattle me to the core.

- I could go home to my family and feel present instead of distracted and stressed by what might be happening (or not happening) in my absence.

- I could give my time to opportunities and challenges that gave me energy, instead of leaving every day feeling drained.

And I wanted my team at my side. I didn't want to build it alone.

Ultimately, the gift and the burden, as you sort through the personal shit, is this: you can only solve the problems in the business as you are able to address the problems of your own leadership. This requires an immense amount of courage, honesty, and risk.

Courage to show up honestly, deal with reality, and demonstrate vulnerability.

Accept risk. Give yourself permission to fail with the belief that there is a better way forward.

Embrace possibility. Suspend your disbelief. Deliberately move forward despite your fear.

Are you willing?

*"Vulnerability is not winning or losing; it's having the courage to show up and be seen when we have no control over the outcome. Vulnerability is not weakness; it's our greatest measure of courage."* —Brene Brown

**It starts by answering these three
imperative questions honestly:**

- **Who is my audience?** Who we live our lives for. Who we give permission to judge our life.

- **Why do I matter?** Our significance is derived from what we think our audience thinks of us.

- **Who am I?** This is our identity; where our significance is derived and it's based on what our audience tells us.

What comes up for you as you think about these three questions? How do you feel?

Is it true?

Coming to your answers for these questions is a process. I know I've been on this journey for 10+ years. Here's a few resources that helped me go deeper.

- *The Only Leaders Worth\* Following* by Tim Spiker

- *Leadership and Self-Deception* by The Arbinger Institute

- *Dare to Lead* by Brene Brown

I really believe that Renegades have a special call to lead in a way that very few are called to. It requires a rare level of belief and tenacity. The stakes are usually higher and more risky than most are able to handle—the potential for failure is just as great, if not greater than the potential to succeed.

But we know that's how great visions are realized.

# Chapter 3

# THE GROUNDWORK

## YOUR CREW

The mistake we make is when we start isolating ourselves and begin believing that in order to get where we want to go, the only way is to go alone. You can move a lot faster on your own. You are only accountable to you.

But it's also true that no great hero does it alone.

There's a ceiling to what you can and will do as a lone wolf. You're likely feeling the pain of that right now as Chief Everything Officer. You may have even been burned once or twice when you tried to invite people in.

But what we both know is that a business at scale requires a collective of willing, caring, and trustworthy people to continue to scale.

It's not about getting warm bodies in the room to spitball an idea or carry out your plans.

**It's about building a crew of trusted
people to surround yourself with.**

These people should not only be invested in helping realize
the success in the business, but they should be invested in
you, too. They should want to see and help *you* succeed.
That requires a level of commitment, maturity, and candor
that not everyone can give you, but should be a baseline
expectation for anyone who is a part of this team.

The formula I've used for building out my crew is this:

1. Function

2. Values alignment

3. F.I.T.

**Function**

The role they play in your crew is clear. Expectations, boundaries, and commitments are set. I would recommend finding partners in these categories.

### Leadership Team

If you're fighting a war or slaying a dragon, these are your generals; your knights at the round table. They are dedicated to the vision and motivated to help you build and execute the strategy to make it happen.

They are commanding the departments or major functions of your business and should represent the most essential parts of what keeps your business running. Very often at the start, those people represent the three most basic functions of any business: Commerce (how you make money), Capacity (how you deliver on your product/service), and Capital (managing financial and human resources) functions of your business.

Most businesses are only slightly more complicated than that. The benefit of this team is that they have such clear responsibility and expectations that they operate with a high level of autonomy and can be trusted to have candid, honest conversations about results.

## Operator

This is your right-hand. The Robin to your Batman.
They are the brakes. You are the gas.

The person you're looking for is the person who can play opposite to your every Renegade impulse. They are usually logical, planned, and skeptical. They like order and process. And maybe most of all, they can get shit done. They ensure confident execution and regulate steady progress on key initiatives in your business. They are essential to building in the consistency and sustainability you need to grow past the stage you're currently in.

The beauty in this partner is their ability to free you up to continue being the Renegade you are while they protect the business you are building. And they provide the freedom for **you** to no longer need to be this regulating figure in the business.

They are the buffer between you and the rest of your business to help keep you from setting fire to progress as Renegades are prone to do. They are a healthy protector. They are an ally in all important decisions. They will give you the hard facts and the realities of what's in front of you, but they will also be the first to initiate a way to make your vision come to life. Their focus on execution today allows you the mental space to think big picture, years ahead, and into spaces your business has yet to touch.

## Admin

It might seem obvious or oversimplified to say it, but you need an assistant. Most Renegades suck at the details. And if you think you're not one of them… maybe ask around. The return on your time will multiply when you stop spending half of your day sorting through your inbox and calendar and give it to someone who is 50x better at it. They will give you the margin you need to spend your brain cells on your gifts to create and innovate on a larger scale instead of getting lost in the details. Tell them where you want to spend your time and let them figure it out.

## Coach

This is your Mr. Miyagi. The person who passes along wisdom from their own journey. They are usually 10 or 20 or 40 years ahead of you in life. The wisest thing we can do on the journey is ask the person on the road coming back what's up ahead. You're giving this person permission to guide you, correct you, and teach you. Their core objective should be to help you and invest in you.

## Peer Group

These people are your allies. They are the ones you've made pacts with to protect and support one another in the fray. They might be in the same boat as you, endeavoring from Renegade-Founder to Renegade-Leader, or they may be slightly ahead or behind you. The goal in having these partners is camaraderie, knowledge-sharing, and creating a safe place for you to work out all the shit that comes your way as a business leader.

## Values Alignment

Your crew should be individuals who are actively on the journey to become inwardly sound and others focused. Even if they have miles to go, the intention and dedication to their own growth should be apparent.

This is essential. The idea is for this crew to come alongside you. You should not be dragging them along or questioning their motives.

In conjunction, we should be inviting people with whom we have real trust.

In *The Five Dysfunctions of a Team*, Patrick Lencioni explains "Trust is the foundation of real teamwork."

And when we don't have it we may not be at each other's throats, but any kind of harmony is merely artificial.

You can't have artificial harmony to grow and scale in a healthy environment. You can't afford it for where you want to go.

We should always be able to answer these four questions about the people we let into our inner circle:

**1.** Can I trust this person to care about me?

**2.** Can I trust this person to be competent — to know what they are talking about?

**3.** Can I trust this person to be dependable and keep their promises?

**4.** Can I trust this person to respect me?

Usually the leaders I work with have no trouble identifying when trust is low or absent with someone key in their inner circle. The hard part is addressing it. Sometimes the people in your life now assume a role close to your business that is not deserved or will not help you move forward. If you're going to scale, these people cannot come with you.

Being a Renegade-Leader requires your candid and whole-hearted being. You have to be able to completely trust this team. If there is any fear that they can't or won't show up for you and for the business, or if there's an impulse to control and micromanage how they contribute, then they either don't belong in your circle or you need to look inward at what keeps you from trusting them completely.

It doesn't have to be a dramatic break up, and it's probably not a great idea to start with "you are untrustworthy," but it does need to be addressed sooner rather than later in this shift you're making. It's imperative to not only get trustworthy leaders in your midst, but to remove untrustworthy people from influencing what's ahead of you.

## F.I.T.

If we can ensure that they are trustworthy leaders and understand the functions we need within our inner circle, then the last element is knowing if they are a F.I.T.

> Does this role **Fuel** their Unique Genius?

> Can they make a significant, positive **Impact** for you and with you?

> Is it **Timely** for them and for you? Think about their stage of life, the stage of business you're in, capacity, trajectory, and maturity. Is it the right time?

If you can't answer with a resounding YES to all three...
PAUSE. Think it through. It's much harder to uninvite these
people from these important roles in your inner circle. Protect
it, protect yourself, and the business you're building toward.

When you get the right people around you to help you in
these key areas, you will clarify your priorities. You will make
room for the Renegade-Leader in you while building the
guardrails you need to stay the course and continually bring
out the best in you and the business you're building.

There's no skipping this step to scale. And for some Renegades
this is perhaps the most challenging change of all. People =
immediate complexity. People = pacing in a new way. Keep in
mind how much of a shift this will be for you from autonomy and
decide now if you're willing and able to sync up with the pack.

Chapter 4

# THE MYTH

One last note on values alignment and F.I.T. that is often
overlooked: there is a really good chance your Renegade-
Founder disposition leads you to mistrust your own contribution.

You're reading this book right now because perhaps there
is some question in your mind about this work you're doing
fueling your genius, allowing you to create the impact you
want to see, and being timely for where you want to go.
Maybe you can't help but feel like this is a beast of your own
making and you might be the villain behind it all. A myth may
begin to seed itself in your mind that ultimately you need
to get out of the way and find a hobby to keep you from
meddling in the stability and structure your business needs.

Before we move on, I need you to set that myth aside if it's
ringing in your head. The opposite is actually true for the
businesses I and my fellow coaches have been able to help.

The truth is, you're the linchpin in the organization. There is nowhere near the forward motion, innovation, clarity of vision, or depth of soul than what lies within you. In the next several chapters, I'm going to share a handful of shifts I've made successfully that not only prove that this myth is just a myth, but also demonstrate how key you are to the future of your organization. Think of yourself in the next few chapters as the architect.

For you to build the business you want to see and have the freedom you want to have, you have been charged with designing a new model using some existing parts.

# 5: The

Chapter 5

# THE BIG SIX

The goal is not to take yourself out of the important decisions or remove your influence over the direction the business goes. It's also never worked in my experience to force a bunch of new rules and restrictions on Renegade-Founders like us. We need boundaries, but we don't want to box ourselves in. We shouldn't have to, but most solutions you've likely encountered want to force systems in place and create rigid structures that kill the Renegade spirit that makes you YOU and the business what it is.

So what kind of rules create systems to scale without encroaching on your freedom?

They don't, and they won't.

However, shifting your mindset gives you both.

In this chapter, I'm going to give you six simple shifts that helped me move from Renegade-Founder to Renegade-Leader. These are decisions you get to make, not rules that are imposed. If anything, they are minimally giving you a frame to design your dream on.

What I can tell you is that practicing these principles helped me better focus and direct the unique power I have as a Renegade. It stopped me from being an arsonist and empowered someone else, someone I could trust, to own these six shifts. It directed my time to spend it more often on the vision and future. It stopped me from getting bogged down in the details, the minutiae. It empowered the smart, trustworthy people on my team to lead better, make moves with more confidence, and own their part with as much clarity as I had about where we were going.

I want to show you how making these intentional choices changed the game for me and a lot of the business owners I've worked with over the last decade. They've all moved from the lonely position of being a Renegade-Founder to running growing organizations with a team of senior leaders.

These shifts will become the foundation for how your team thinks, moves, acts, and decides. It will start with you and it will continue with them. Keep that in mind as you think about the shifts you need to make.

And just to set your mind at ease… making these shifts is never permanent and rarely fall into place all at once. You're not deciding a new fate, you're just making decisions to shape a preferred future. There's still lots of room for improvisation, innovation, and risk. The shift is all about extending impact beyond just you and into a bigger arena. Remember, it's a fight for dignity.

This is the start of seeing what happens when you become the Renegade-Leader your business needs.

# THE BIG SIX

## SHIFT #1: THE DESIGN SHIFT

*"Never be limited by other people's limited imaginations."* —Mae Jemison

I grew up in a fairly conservative, lower-middle class family in rural Ohio. My dad was a pastor and my mom took care of all of us.

As it is with a lot of families in ministry work, we always ate well and had what we needed, but we didn't have a lot of extras. My parents were very careful when it came to spending money— we went out to eat once a year, went on vacation once a year, and my mom even made some of my clothes to save on new shirts and pants as I grew. They were also careful not to waste anything that still had value.

My mom taught us that anything can be done with the resources you have on hand. Her shorthand way of saying this to me and my siblings was "mud and spit." Jesus healed the blind man in the gospels with what he had available around him: dirt and spit.

In reality, what this looked like for teenage-Benj was less a miracle and more finding work-arounds for the things I couldn't afford or activities I wasn't allowed to do.

For example, when I was in high school my parents were fairly strict about letting me go to parties at houses of families they didn't know. They also didn't regularly have a budget for me to invite a bunch of my friends over, feed everyone and keep them entertained. So... "mud and spit" sparked one of my first entrepreneurial ideas. I looked around and realized that our empty, 20,000 square-foot barn, a strobe light, the boombox I had in my room, and my playstation would make for a pretty decent place to hang out with my friends. I could charge a fee for snacks, and invite whoever I wanted. It became a new hang out for all my friends and kept me from spending my weekends at home alone.

Now, in all honesty, whenever we are told to
"work with what you've got," it sucks.

Believe me, I rolled my eyes at my mom's "mud and spit" mantra for a long time before it sunk in and I saw how valuable that thinking was for my journey as an entrepreneur. (Thanks, mom)

It helped me leverage and grow the resources I had in businesses that had next to nothing.

It helped me train my businesses to reach profitability sooner than if I'd outfitted every problem with traditional solutions. That kind of thinking forced me to overcome a barrier that most people are not willing to push past. The gift of the Renegade is having the tenacity to keep pushing an idea forward regardless of immediate resources. Maybe like me, you've learned there is so much more value in discovering the way around than being handed the "out of the box" solution.

Maybe like me, you grew up being told
to "play the hand you're dealt."

The difference for Renegades like us is that they
don't settle in and get used to the circumstances.
They come back with, "I'll bet on myself."

So many people fear the messes that come with pursuing possibility, and determine that the risk is far greater than the reward. But the Renegade knows better. They run *into* the mess full speed because we know that the sooner, faster, and harder we run into the mess, the sooner we learn. The risk of failure is nothing weighed against the risk of regret.

For Renegades, the status quo ceases to matter.
Failure is a requirement. Everything has room
for reinvention. Because they know…

## …designing any future requires disruption.

The garage start-up stories about funding an idea with almost
nothing more than resilience and an insane amount of belief
are so common in the world of Renegades. So many of them
fought ridiculous odds, pushed past slammed doors, and
ensured years of doubt from the people closest to them to get
where they are. Sara Blakely, founder of Spanx, is one of my
favorite examples of this kind of radical, self-motivated bet.

"We'd sit around the dinner table and [my dad would] ask,
'What did you guys fail at this week?' If we had nothing to tell
him, he'd be disappointed," she said. "He knew that many
people become paralyzed by the fear of failure. My father
wanted us to try everything and feel free to push the envelope.
His attitude taught me to define failure as not trying something
I want to do instead of not achieving the right outcome."

Sarah definitely heard him loud and clear.

- She failed the LSAT twice.

- Got turned down for a job wearing a
  Goofy costume at Disney World.

- Landed at a job in Atlanta selling fax
  machines door-to-door.

"It was the kind of place that would hire anyone with a pulse," she said. "On my first day, they handed me a phone book and said, 'Here are your four zip codes. Now get out there and sell.' There was no list of accounts that were likely to buy from me. I had to 100 percent drum up my own leads. Most doors were slammed in my face. I saw my business card ripped up at least once a week, and I even had a few police escorts out of buildings."

Nevertheless, Sarah learned she was good at selling. She knew she wanted to work for herself someday and this was a training ground. Then, on a day when she needed a way to make a pair of white pants fit better, she discovered shapewear, and knew what it would take to sell it.

"Everybody has a multimillion-dollar idea inside them," she says. "Edison said, 'Genius is one percent inspiration and 99 percent perspiration.' The same holds true for innovation, invention, and entrepreneurship."

We kept pushing when everyone else stops.

That's the Renegade way.

## THE SHIFT

All that being said, I would challenge us to not to stop here and reminisce on all of the ways we've poured our sweat and blood for the survival of the business. While we've all done amazing, ridiculous, impossible things to breathe life into our work, we have to remember that no one is self-made. If they are, you will probably never hear of them.

There is an existing design in every organization and then there is an intentional one. In a self-made business, the founder stays at the center of the universe and acts as a gravitational pull for everything. You've probably heard it said, **"Your business is already finely tuned for the results it is** *currently* **getting"**. That could be a welcome result, but more often than not, it's less than optimal.

It's limiting you from doing anything in your Renegade wheelhouse.
It's keeping everyone confused about how to contribute.
It's placing a ceiling on your growth potential.

If we want to grow and see the business at scale, we have to help our organization move beyond the barriers and think bigger than the cards on the table. You are likely a master of betting on the right people or right ideas to fuel growth in your organization, but the shift we have to make is one that brings clarity and intention to how we make bets, how to think strategically about the next move, and stay one step ahead.

SHIFT  #/

THE WORLD SAYS

~~"Play the hand you're dealt."~~

BUT YOU SAID

~~"I'll bet on myself."~~

THE *Design*

SAYS

*Bet with*

SHIFT

INTENTION.

# THE DESIGN SHIFT

~~"Play the hand you're dealt."~~
~~"I'll bet on myself."~~
**The design shift:** Bet with intention.

The shift isn't meant to be prescriptive about every decision or activity in the business. It's simply having clear intent where most organizations don't.

- 7 out of 10 employees are misaligned with their company's strategic direction.

- 55% of managers can only name one of their companies top five priorities.

- 42% of employees say they are not engaged in any training for adopting process techniques.

**I've found that designing with intent starts in three key areas:**

- **Your organizational structure** - determining the functions and the right people for the roles the business needs most. Yeah, including you.

- **Your most-repeatable processes** - don't freak out. It doesn't need to be complex or organized in a four-inch binder. You just need a known, repeatable way of doing key activities so that everyone can be smart with their time and effort. There might be ten ways to skin a cat, pick yours and write it down.

- **Your strategic bets** - you have to take risks to make progress. But your bets should be strategic, drawing you closer to the vision you have for the years ahead of you.

Designing these areas with intentionality accomplished a few outcomes for me right out of the gate in my own businesses:

- Created clarity for how work was done and who was actually responsible.

- Made my visionary goals and top priorities known to my team. Even better, my goals and bets became OUR goals and bets.

- Redefined the value I could bring to my business when I wasn't wearing every hat.

I want to show you how this works.

My friend Haley Devlin did not start out as Renegade-Founder, but as an incredible partner and Operator for one. In the years since I've known her, she's gone from reigning in a Renegade to becoming an amazing Renegade-Leader in her own right. These are her words about what making this choice did for her and her team at Stratasan—a healthcare technology company founded in Nashville, TN.

## TAKE IT FROM A RENEGADE:

*Haley Devlin*

Partner, DNA Partners

*Early on, we looked and acted very much like a startup, like a small business that didn't really have plans to scale.*

*Today—11 years in and with nearly 100 employees—I feel like we are truly a platform. A platform to build a truly scalable, financially viable company that, potentially, another group would want to pay a lot of dollars for.*

*We've made a massive leap from where we were three or four years ago. One of the problems we were facing back then was that we just did not have the right people in the right seats, and we didn't have a really good way to evaluate that or even a common language to use around it.*

*We didn't understand how critical this was to the viability of the organization and we had no framework to solve for it. There was also a lack of accountability. People weren't clear on what they were supposed to be doing and their teams weren't clear on it either. They didn't know what was expected of them and how they'd be deemed successful.*

*This created a situation where power was concentrated at the top and our founder Jason had to be involved in a lot more decisions.*

*Today, we have a fully fleshed out leadership team - with the right leaders - and there is clear ownership and accountability of who owns what. Having the right people in those key leadership seats has a profound trickle down effect on the business' ability to be successful.*

*Departments are aligned strategically, tactically, and culturally. We grew 3x in 3 years and I don't think we could have done it without making some of those difficult decisions.*

*Now, Jason is our coach and our visionary and he guides company strategy. Once he's set the strategy, he can leave the functional decision-making to the leadership team.*

After a few years of working together to reorganize their business, Haley and her partner Jason got the offer Haley predicted. They sold their company in 2022 for 150 million — 10x the valuation they expected just a few years before. I also got the joy of seeing their team first-hand learn to think and lead their work with the intentions and bets the business was pursuing as a whole.

The horsepower they gained when everyone in their organization was clear about how to strategically play their part, was apparent, not only in the results they started to see, but in how energized they were to be accountable to the team. Betting with intention pays off.

**YOUR TURN:**
A lot of the choices you need to make require some deep thinking — on your own and also with your crew. A few questions to ask as you think it over:

- **Clear Structure** - what functions can this business not survive without? What will we need from these roles to scale?

- **Repeatable Processes** - are we reinventing the wheel? How do we know what's working and what needs improving?

- **Strategic Bets** - Do we actually know the #1 goal or outcome we want as an organization? How far can we get in one year? What do we need to focus on in order to get there?

*"It is not the critic who counts; not the man who points out how the strong man stumbles, or where the doer of deeds could have done them better. The credit belongs to the man who is actually in the arena, whose face is marred by dust and sweat and blood; who strives valiantly; who errs, who comes short again and again, because there is no effort without error..."*
—Theodore Roosevelt, Citizenship Within A Republic

## SHIFT #2: THE CADENCE SHIFT

*"Entrepreneurs: the only people who work 80 hours a week to avoid working 40 hours a week for someone else."* —Lori Greiner, Shark Tank

The "right" move for most people is the safe one. Predictable. Low-risk. Familiar territory.

There are, of course, good reasons for this. We want to protect our livelihoods, our families, and our future options. Plus, there's a blueprint here in Western culture that's supposedly designed to help us reach the ever-elusive American Dream. →→→→→→

~~Be a good student~~ → get into a good college → find a good job → work your way up the ladder to a secure position in a good company → put 10% of your earnings in a 401k → retire at 65 → say you've had a good life.

(If you think about it… even this "certain" path to success is an unsure bet.)

Oh, and if you want to avoid absolute failure…. DON'T:

- Quit school

- Take a job without good benefits

- Leave your career path to try something new

- Take too much vacation time

- Disagree or question the boss

- Have gaps in your resume

- Get distracted with a side hustle

- Invest in anything riskier than a 401k

The problem for Renegades is when the "right" steps start to choke out the most true, alive parts of who they are. Not to mention, they start looking around and notice that what everyone else is doing is just F**KING BORING!

My business partner Chris White knows the risk in breaking this mold more than most. He's a third generation entrepreneur, but he didn't jump in feet-first like his family members did in earlier generations. Here's how he tells it.

# IT'S
# F\*\*KING
*boring.*

## TAKE IT FROM A RENEGADE:
*Chris White*
Co-Founder, System & Soul

*"I grew up in an entrepreneurial family. My grandfather and my father started and ran their own businesses for decades. It gave them a sense of freedom and control I think. And my dad was able to provide for our big family just as well as he could have with any other job. But even as a kid, I can remember noticing how the business took a toll on him. There were a lot of moments I can remember my dad being absent from the sidelines of my basketball and football games when I was growing up. And when he was there or at home with our family—like most entrepreneurs— we could tell his mind was often still at work.*

*During my sophomore year at college, my parents decided to sell the company to one of my brothers and they held the note. In short order, my brother failed miserably running the company and my parents had to shut it down. They ended up with nothing in their retirement years. It was devastating. All that work, all that sacrifice.*

*So when it came time for me to pick my career path, the best course of action I could see to avoid a similar fate was to get a safe job in a big, stable company. I landed a sales position with a Motorola distributor and stayed there for a decade doing what I thought was the safest job I could ask for.*

*The problem was it kept me on the road nearly every week of the year, and when I started to think about what really got me excited about my work, I realized what I was doing was just making me restless for something more. I wanted a challenge, something I could build on my own, and build the life I wanted at the same time. I was also missing so much of my kid's lives being on the road, and I started to dream about building something for myself like my grandparents and parents did.*

*I finally decided it was time to make a move. I saved up a year's worth of my salary before I quit my job, and started my own business. At the time, I had no idea if it would work out, but I was going to give it a year and see what I could do on my own. From then on, I knew I woke up every day with a fire under my ass to make sure I gave it my all, and I can honestly say, it's the best decision I could have made.*

*Since I took that leap, I've started and sold four companies, and have been a business coach for over a decade to hundreds of leadership teams. The work I do is incredibly rewarding. I'd say the most important thing I've learned over the years is that settling for good enough doesn't usually require much risk. It's when we dream about that next level of freedom, progress, and possibility that we must be ready to jump head first into the unknown. I can't describe a more exciting, well-lived life than that."*

For Renegade-Founders the drive to **die on adventure** is so much stronger than to **live in the rat race**.

And while that doesn't guarantee we hit a home run every time, one thing for sure is that our work is never boring.

I've had my fair share of "off key" decisions and ventures that have made certain people in my life raise their eyebrows. And when they did, I couldn't and didn't waste any time trying to prove my way was better or more rewarding. I just followed through on what I knew I needed for the rhythm of my life and totally gave in to what mattered to me.

Like Chris described, we reach a point when the bet on ourselves feels more sure and true than letting anyone else decide our fate. And the dividends we see when they make that bet—win or lose—teaches us more and gives us more freedom than the safe track ever could.

## THE SHIFT

The shift I had to make in my own journey to becoming a true Renegade-Leader was not tamping down my drive or giving into convention. I had to learn how to pace my off-beat thinking with the people who were holding to the bassline. I learned that they needed me to push us beyond what we were comfortable doing, and I needed them to keep us together and ensure that as we took risks and pushed forward into new territory, they could keep the rest of the business in sync.

The people around us used to say as a warning of the failures ahead, "don't quit your day job."

And of course as Founders we said, "thank you, but I'll dance to the beat of my own drum." As Renegade-Founders we've thrived by running out ahead, doing a big explosive musical number on our own, leaving the slowpokes in the dust and the chorus backstage.

But as Leaders, the second shift we need to make is to learn to set the bassline and improvise with the band as a whole.

In jazz music there's an emphasis on creating as you go, improvising, and surprising not only the audience but the band with a new challenge to take on. When we listen to jazz we tend to hear that improvisation over everything else. But beneath it, moving the song forward evenly and steadily, is the bassline.

I love the way Ornette Coleman describes this simultaneously wild, and balanced approach, *"Jazz is the only music in which the same note can be played night after night but differently each time."*

Improvisation is just noise if we don't ground ourselves in the bassline. And every player, even the most talented virtuoso, respects the bassline.

SHIFT # 2

THE WORLD SAYS

~~"Don't quit your day job.~~

BUT YOU SAID

~~"I'll dance to the beat~~

THE *Cadence*

SAYS *Set a*

*of your own drum."*

SHIFT

# BASSLINE.

## THE CADENCE SHIFT

Shift #2: "Don't quit your day job."
"I'll dance to the beat of your own drum."
**Set a bassline.**

The very best example I've seen of this in my work as a business coach actually included music and some very unexpected dancing. When I meet with a founder and their team we don't often end up busting moves. As you can imagine, it's not usually on the meeting agenda, but in one case it was.

I was in Boston meeting with a senior leadership team for the first time to help them build their annual strategic plan. I'd worked with this team a few times before and they were always very focused and ready to work, so I came in ready to help them find their pace and best initiatives for the coming year.

The morning of the first day was extremely productive—people were engaged, asking great questions, and coming to really profound insights. They were thinking critically and so clearly and intently engaged in designing the future of the business. We planned to break for lunch around noon and then jump back into the conversation. I was feeling just as eager as they were all morning to get back to work and pick up where we'd left off, so I announced a five-minute warning to transition back into our work and started looking over my notes. As time ticked down and the people in the room tossed their lunch plates, someone cranked a stereo and without hesitation the whole room started dancing. They were jumping, cabbage patching, and mouthing the words as if this interruption was just part of some strange routine or a well-rehearsed prank on me.

When the song ended everyone sat back down and looked at me, ready to get back to work.

I was definitely confused, and almost certain I was being punked.

So, I asked them what just happened,
and what they said floored me.

They dance every time they are together. Same song. Same silly moves. Same group of serious, smart executives. They don't do it to be cool or trendy. They're not a professional dance troupe. And even if they feel like they don't want to, they do it anyway.

It's a habit that draws their team together and kills any ego,
and serves as a reminder to anyone pushing their own
agenda—we pace together. They use this dance to get on
the same page, and quite literally move at the same pace.

The shift we have to make as a Renegade-Leader is to
set the bassline for our organization and hold it steady.

The Cadence Shift requires you to build recurring touch points to hold the whole organization accountable to the goals that are set, and connect the team back to the values you set. While Renegades love to improv, most people thrive in predictability. We can have both, it's just a matter of being intentional.

In setting the bassline for my teams, I learned to set
rhythms to the workflow that gave everyone:

**1.** Clear milestones, feedback loops, and touchpoints
on their work and the outcomes I expected

**2.** Sacredly held space to voice challenges,
share ideas and stay connected

**3.** Freedom from the tyranny of the urgent, the shiny
objects, and the new most important priority.

Like dancing together, the habits I learned to set with my team became practical ways to not only pace the work we were doing, but also give them the dignity of forward momentum. I stopped calling them on the phone at random. I stopped hijacking conversations in meetings to share my latest ideas. And I could tell that they not only accomplished more and achieved better results, but they felt involved, proactive and a part of the work they were doing, not just reactive to the next most important thing.

**Here's three simple ways I've made this work:**

- **We set Quarterly Objectives:** we set 90-day project goals to move major initiatives forward that impact the one-year focus and long-term destination of the organization.

- **We hold Weekly Sync meetings (for every team, always, every week, no exceptions, no higher priority):** we meet weekly, same time, same agenda to check on progress, review objectives, remove obstacles, and discuss opportunities. Everyone has a voice and more of often than not, as the Founder, I'm there to listen. We've also successfully eliminated hundreds of other wasted hours meeting sporadically.

- **We invite everyone into "Health F.I.T." Conversations:** Every manger of people meets one-on-one with team members every three months to check-in on performance, talk about their personal and professional goals, how we can help them get there, and ultimately build trust and demonstrate that this kind of focused pace can not only help us with our business initiatives, but help our people do the things they dream of doing in their lives.

These three repeated patterns form the bassline supporting every part of the businesses I've founded and coached. It's really not rocket science, but it's difficult (especially for us Renegades) because it requires some of the discipline and consistency that we tend to avoid. I think what you'll find in trying some of these things is more freedom, more buy-in, more ideas getting launched, and more time spent on the biggest bets in your business.

Reminder: You can delegate the management of this cadence in order to make sure it happens consistently.

## TAKE IT FROM A RENEGADE:
### David McMillian
President, McMillian & Associates

*In the past I've been somewhat of an if-I-see-a-shiny-object-I'm-going-to-go-that-direction kind of person.*

*I would say early in my business there was a lack of consistency and then, maybe, a lack of like predictability coming from the top, or at least amongst the leadership team. And I think partly that's because we didn't have a system.*

*There was not a lot of predictability around the focus of the business because it was driven by what my focus was at the moment—and that can change very easily. If something was right in front of my face and driving my attention from a sales or a client perspective or a technology perspective, that's what drove the organization. We didn't have cohesion either. Even if I felt like I had a clear direction and I was going that direction, we weren't getting there with everybody. We weren't moving with everybody on the same page towards our end goals.*

*I think when you actually take time to carve out and say, "Hey, let's think through what we're working on," and everybody agrees to that focus, there's some collective buy-in and accountability. I think having a habit like that allows you to accomplish a lot more.*

*We get together on a quarterly basis and in the simple habit of meeting quarterly, we build in—not only focused work—but team health. It gives us a consistent way to check in on how things are going.*

*But I know it starts with me. What's that saying? "All organizational problems are leadership problems?" So I know now that whatever problem that we're facing at some level, I've got to own and be accountable.*

—David McMillan, Renegade-Leader

Again, if you can pace these few things well, and empower the team, you should start to feel momentum and the dignity of working in sync on the highest value projects with everyone attuned to their part.

**YOUR TURN:**

There are a couple of actionable ways to begin this shift and practice pacing with your team. Take these prompts and have a conversation with your top leaders.

## For setting Quarterly Objectives:

**Quarterly Objective**     No matter what it takes, at the end of 90 days we must accomplish _____.

**Key Results**     In order to make this happen, I'll need to do _____,

_____,

and _____.

**30-Day Milestone**     30 days from now, I will be able to show _____ as progress toward this goal.

**60-Day Milestone**     60 days from now, I will be able to show _____ as progress toward this goal.

Lastly, if I could make any decisions today that would accelerate this, I would _____.

**Clarify the win before you begin.**

**For Weekly Meetings:**

- When we meet, is the agenda and purpose clear? Are the outcomes defined?

- Are people leaving with assigned actions and due dates with feedback loops? Are the right people involved? (or are too many people involved just because?)

- Connect first, and then spend as much time as possible discussing opportunities.

**Tips from clients who are crushing it:**

- Look across your calendar. Are there meeting blocks that can be combined that include similar topics, or include the same teammates?

  *Example: Can you take 3-4, 30-minute client status meetings and turn them into one 60-minute meeting?*

- Set a "no-meeting day" that protects everyone in the whole company. Block it. Keep it. And watch work get done.

**For one-on-one (Healthy F.I.T.) conversations:**

**On a weekly basis....**
There are 3 questions I ask in my 1-on-1 meetings
to connect, solve problems, and find solutions.

  1. How are you really? (How are you feeling?)

  2. What are you working on?

  3. How can I support you?

The less you say, the more room you give them to surface
feelings, challenges, and areas where they need your help.

**On a quarterly basis...**

We ask team members from the beginning of
their time working with us to create a Personal
Road Map that defines their unique skills, personal
mission, personal and professional goals, and
overall satisfaction and "fit" in their role.

In the quarterly conversation, we review their
Road Map and discuss areas for growth, review
and celebrate performance, and ask where
we as leaders can help them succeed.

Use the QR code to see what that
looks like and access a copy.

**P.S.**

I get it. The idea of executing this is awesome, but overwhelming for someone who hates details. You're in good company. When you start building these habits into the cadence of your business, keep it all in one place. We've built an app to help make this shift ridiculously easy. Check out S2sync.com

# THE BIG SIX

## SHIFT #3: THE SCORE SHIFT

*"If you're prepared and you know what it takes, it's not a risk. You just have to figure out how to get there. There is always a way to get there."* —Mark Cuban

The last boss I ever worked for—let's just call him Kevin—had a very determined approach to the way he did business. His confidence in his ideas outweighed anyone else's opinions. He was critical of anyone else's approach. He micromanaged how projects were done. It truly seemed like he couldn't let anyone or any new thought enter into his business without his identity as the "boss" being threatened. Certainly being the smartest guy in every room was a requirement for his ego to stay intact, so curiosity was always seen as an attack.

At the time I was in my early twenties. I had a lot of ideas and didn't realize how personally offensive all of the questions and opinions I shared with him were. After about two years working with him I knew I wanted to run my own business, and there were also lots of better and different ways to do it than what I was experiencing.

- I wanted to have creative freedom to take my clients projects in directions Kevin would always crush.

- I wanted to say "no" to clients who didn't share my values.

- I wanted to pay myself and my team better than Kevin did.

- I wanted people to like coming to work, building relationships, and growing to be healthier and happier.

- I wanted to be an incredible competitor in my market, not just another agency holding up one guy's ego.

As the Renegade story often goes, my tension with Kevin reached a tipping point. In a heated conversation that clearly wasn't getting any closer to a resolution for either of us, he said, "You're fired," and I said, "I quit." (Big debate on which of those came first.)

When I said those words to Kevin, I didn't have a plan.
I didn't have a book of business I could take with me.
I didn't have a network of peers to help
me land somewhere else easily.
And I'd just torched the one bridge I'd built in my early career.
Awesome.

From the outside, it probably looked thoughtless and impulsive. All I knew was that I needed to do work I could influence and work that really mattered. If I was going to sign my name on something for the rest of my life, I needed to trust what my gut was telling me. Push forward, and figure out the rest.

[Trinity] *"Neo, No One Has Ever Done Anything Like This."*

[Neo] *"That's Why It's Going To Work."*

In that stand-off with Kevin, and in so many other less dramatic moments before that, I felt like I was fighting against the lie that "how things are done is how they should be." Too many times I'd seen certainty get mistaken (and celebrated) as clarity when it's really just narrow thinking. As a Renegade, you know as well as I do that certainty is a myth. If that's the case, what better way to live than to go with your gut?

Every Renegade-Founder endures the stage of their business where they wear a ridiculous number of hats, and push through wildly unpredictable circumstances to find product-market fit, establish a customer base, and get cash-flow positive. Their ability to flex, pivot, and stay scrappy is what allows them to attend to market opportunities before anyone else and quickly recover when an idea fails. You can't believe there's one way or one answer when you're building from the ground up—that's a death sentence. Instead, we stay alert and ready for the next wave. Agile and adept to make your move at any moment.

The mistake most people have made about me and so many other Renegades is that they believe we're purely driven by impulse. What's more often the case though, is that we're driven by clear purpose; we just follow instinct and improvise the steps to achieve it. Author James Clear calls this a "mindset that can handle uncertainty." No amount of planning will eliminate the threat of uncertainty, so Renegades don't waste time trying to predict the future.

# "EVERYONE HAS A PLAN UNTIL THEY GET PUNCHED IN THE *mouth*,"

Mike Tyson is famous for saying, "Everyone has a plan until they get punched in the mouth," which he did better than most boxers ever have in all of history. He had an ever-evolving plan regardless of whether or not he was swinging or taking a hit.

One opponent in his decades of fighting said that Mike's approach and unrivaled success had a lot to do with speed and his ability to respond in the moment.

"In the ring, he was just another boxer who wanted to beat me and in turn I wanted to beat him. But Tyson had the fastest hands, he was a good all-rounder and a brilliant attacker. He was able to multitask by reading my moves and punch at the same time, as well as being able to dodge. His punches came very quick given his size. He was definitely an animal in the ring. He knew what he wanted and went for it; massive determination to win."

That is the Renegade-Founder. Knowing the game. Counting on the punch. Bobbing and weaving from one challenge to the next.

## THE SHIFT

The difference between us and Mike is that we aren't playing a one-to-one game. Maybe we have in the past. I know that when I launched my own agency, it was Benj against the world—and I could barely afford to pay just him! The shift I had to make over time, as my team grew and the challenges we faced expanded beyond my skills set and capacity, was what I call the Score Shift.

As a Renegade-Founder, I'd already defied the well-meant advice to "know what I was getting myself into."

I said, "I'm going with my gut."
To become the Renegade-Leader I wanted to be for our team, I had to learn to help everyone in the business know when we were winning.

SHIFT # 3

THE WORLD SAYS ~~"Know what you're~~

BUT YOU SAID ~~"I'm going with my gut."~~

THE Score

SAYS Know when

getting yourself into."

SHIFT

you're
WINNING.

## SHIFT #3: THE SCORE SHIFT

~~Shift #3: ""Know what you're getting yourself into."~~
~~"I'm going with my gut."~~
**Know when you're winning.**

*If winning isn't everything, why do they keep score?*
—Vince Lombardi

Before now, you might have been able to haphazardly make progress and generate activity in your business because you were directly connected to every aspect, every lever, and every dollar that flowed in and out of it. That's fine. We can't over analyze the experiment when we're still trying to figure out a formula. As a Renegade-Founder, you and I needed to be proactive and rely on our gut to know what worked and what didn't work.

In a growing business there is ever-increasing complexity in how information and the results of the work that's done is communicated and analyzed. You can continue to go with your gut like you used to, but if you do, you end up withholding valuable insight from the rest of your organization and seriously limit the team's ability to create predictable outcomes.

Now, I'm going to ask you a question with an obvious answer.

When is the best time to check the score during any game?

Answer: While you're in the game.

Checking the score helps us know if we're winning and gives us cues to adjust when we aren't.

One of the key choices I had to make was to set a score for the business and measure what mattered.

As the Renegade-Leader, our role is to help the team see the score and understand the game they're playing, when to call a time-out and regroup, and most importantly, when they are winning. Helping them see the score might be one of the most underrated ways to create dignity and champions of our organizations. Because at the end of the day, we all have a desire to know we're doing a good job.

Think about it. The most commonly cited reason for people of any generation, skill level, or industry to leave a job comes down to a single measurable: compensation. When a person's pay is not equal with the value they feel they contribute, it always becomes a conversation.

They are always keeping score (whether you are or not). They know their numbers, the goals and outcomes they are looking for outside of their role too, and how their paycheck helps them get there. It's a key motivator and a key detractor for people at every level.

If this is the case, why wouldn't we give them indicators that demonstrate success or improvement in everything they do?

My friend and fellow Renegade-Leader, Jonathan Reynolds, explains, "Everyone always seems to expect 100% of their paycheck, so I make sure everyone is 100% clear on the expectations I have for them to earn it." Let them see what results drive goals and outcomes for the business. Let them see their results drive reward, recognition, satisfaction, and maybe even some bigger numbers on those paychecks.

The score is different in every business, but the outcomes should be the same regardless of the industry you're in or the size and scope of the organization:

- clarity for individuals about how they measure their contribution

- clarity for teams on what success looks like as they make bets to drive their role in the business forward

- clarity for the organization on what matters most in what we're aiming to accomplish AND finding ways to predict greater outcomes

The score shift is as much a reflection of the results the business drives as it is about creating dignity for every team member and customer that business serves.

## TAKE IT FROM A RENEGADE:

### Andrew Louder
Founder and CEO of Louder Co.

*We've doubled in size in just the last year plus and it would have been an incredibly chaotic experience if it wasn't for System & Soul. Jonathan King is our System & Soul Coach. He's done so much to help coordinate our efforts.*

*We now meet as a leadership team to identify our quarterly objectives and key results, we meet annually, to set our annual plan, our three-year plan, and our 10-year plan. And then we have what's called our S2 Sync meeting every week where we review our scoreboard of metrics, key performance indicators— things that are keeping the pulse on the business.*

*A big metric for us is something we call "raving fans," which are CEOs or client teams that, you know, for starters, we try to wow them at every step of the way and we try to go above and beyond solving problems that they didn't even know existed.*

*And ultimately, these people become great raving fans, referral sources. They talk us up. Oftentimes we'll talk to prospects and they say, "Hey, can I talk to any of your past clients and see what it's like working with you?" And we say, "Absolutely!"*

*Right away we can give them a slew of numbers and emails that you can reach out to.*

*These things I think have really helped shape us internally and made us better consultants and a really great place to work.*

The kind of clarity Andrew and his team have found around performance indicators gives the team two imperative things:

**1.** A company-wide focus on what drives growth (referrals)

**2.** Confidence, focus, and dignity for each person's role to put their effort and intention behind driving more raving fans

As a Renegade-Leader, you're not just calculating the next move to win another day or another month of business. You're teaching the team how to value every win that comes their way.

**YOUR TURN:**

Start now. Track weekly. Evaluate, add, and subtract as needed over time. You and the team will be so much more clear on what matters and why.

**If you're ready to begin sketching this out, here are six tips that will help you get started building a simple, powerful Scoreboard to review with your team:**

1. Start measuring and reviewing key performance indicators on a weekly basis.

2. Assign ONE clear owner who is responsible for updating the scoreboard and driving outcomes.

3. Tie in key performance indicators to each person's role in the organization.

4. Measure one metric that indicates progress toward long-term goals or your company's destination.

5. Measure one metric tied to what drives
your company's economic engine.*

6. Remember, great metrics tell us what will happen,
not what happened. It's better to measure
the right activities that drive results.

**Bonus thought:** Someone once told me, "for any team member,
you can always measure speed, quality, and capacity."

**Examples to get you started:**

Company Measurables:
- Lifetime value of a client
- % of Profit
- # of Companies or Customers served
- # of Referrals given

Team or Individual Measurables:
- # of Products purchased
- # of New clients gained per week
- Customer support response time
- % of Profit per order shipped

*Economic engine is the one thing that generates revenue
growth in your business. The thing you want to measure
is likely not the economic engine directly, but what
drives the engine. If you put more fuel in the tank so the
engine could keep running, what would that fuel be?
Ex. # of leads in a pipeline, # of repeat customers.

# THE BIG SIX

## SHIFT #4: THE DESTINATION SHIFT

*"History will be kind to me for I intend to write it."*
—Winston Churchill

In September 2009, my wife and I brought our first-born son home from the hospital. I was several years into running my own business at that point, and this next week would be the longest amount of time I would have taken away from my work in years. No sooner had we gotten all the bags and our new baby out of the car and into the house when the phone rang.

I assumed it would be one of our parents or siblings calling to welcome us home, but it wasn't. It was Jeff, the one full-time graphic designer that I had working for me at the time. He was calling to get my feedback on a very important project we'd been working on for the NFL. This was a HUGE opportunity for us at the time and a rare project from an organization of that size given to a tiny agency like mine.

Knowing how big a deal this was for our business, I stepped away briefly from my wife and our day-old son to check my email and quickly review his work. What I thought would be routine adjustments and easy approval turned into a nightmare. Jeff had completely bombed this project. Nothing about it was right. He'd completely missed the big picture I had in mind, and now time was running out.

I couldn't send the work back for him to re-do at that point and there was no one else to call for help. I knew it was all on me. I had to start over and rebuild our whole project from scratch.

Instead of enjoying the first three days of my son's life and adjusting as new parents, I spent nearly all 72 hours in front of my computer trying to recreate the work and make the deadline.

For the first five years of running my agency, there were a lot of moments like that. But eventually, the business grew and I was able to get more of the right people in place. As my team expanded, I was optimistic that I would free myself up to do more of what I hoped to be doing 5 years ago—thinking about our next 5 years and how to get there. But that's not what happened. I wasn't literally on-call 24 hours a day anymore, but I was mentally on-call.

I traded tasks for endless questions from the team.
I traded time working on projects for time in endless meetings.
I traded doing it myself for trying to manage madness.

And I knew this wasn't getting us where we wanted to be down the road.

Ultimately, I felt like I was losing track of the future of the business I'd envisioned in the first place. And even worse, I had a relentless voice in my head saying, "Work like there is someone working 24 hours a day to take it all away from you."

I was spending every waking moment churning through ideas, problems, and opportunities. The business and all of its needs followed me everywhere: into the shower, into my dreams, into my road-trip conversation with my wife, into family vacations, and into any quiet moment I might have.

If you've been in this season as a Renegade-Founder, then you've likely been asked by someone: "Why would you want to work this hard (especially when you're not even getting paid well)?"

It's hardly worth trying to explain to these people that as Renegades, we just know that this mental grind is part of what it takes to get where we dream of being.

Most people hedge their bets, believing, if you're patient, you might get lucky. But Renegades know that you have to show up for "luck" to find you. Better yet, you get lucky when you make your own luck.

One of my favorite examples of this kind of tenacity began with a bunch of college bros in the mid 2000's. Tyler Toney and his housemates killed time between classes and on weekends playing hockey in their living room of their townhouse and attempting impossible trick shots in the backyard.

A spontaneous bet led the guys to make a video montage of outrageous basketball shots, which they titled "Dude Perfect" and posted on an emerging platform called YouTube (ever heard of it?).

That first video wound up on *Good Morning America* and launched a new series of outrageous stunts the guys set out to pull off: an impossible shot from the third tier of a football stadium to the 50 yard line, a here-goes-nothing lob from the door of a plane mid-flight into a hoop thousands of feet below, and so on. They started trending online and years later they've completed hundreds of stunts that have earned them more than a combined 15 BILLION video views.

This crew of college buddies created one of the all-time most popular channels on Youtube and they now run a growing multi-million dollar media company. But the business of impressive trick shots was not built on luck. Tyler was quoted saying, "You know, everybody always says it's the easiest and most fun job in the world. It's definitely the most fun, but it's not the easiest." They learned, like other Renegades, that the decisions that would drive them forward couldn't be practiced hundreds of times before they nailed it. They only had—at most—a couple of shots.

It was a GRIND. It took *Dude Perfect* five grueling years of trying to build ad revenue and establish brand sponsorships while juggling their day jobs before their YouTube popularity turned into a legit business. And now they are expanding into all kinds of different revenue streams including the building of a Dude Perfect theme park.

I love their example because it's real—even for some of the best known internet celebrities. No one gets exempt from showing up to make luck a reality.

What I think we have to realize, though, is that it's not just grinding. It's not just luck that pushes a business to the next level of growth or success. There will be some elements of both of those things, but I think the magic that sustains a team for all the months or years of working toward something is having a compelling reason to keep pushing toward their destination.

## THE SHIFT

As I coach teams and work in my own businesses as a Renegade, I've learned it's imperative to communicate the long view to every person in an organization—even if they are perfectly content to keep grinding away.

If we don't, we all so easily lose sight of why what we do matters. We become reactive. We make decisions and measure our business on a very short time horizon.

Up until now, the goal or a vision that drove you forward likely relied on sheer tenacity, luck you've had, or clever moves you could make to leap forward. I see a lot of Renegade-Founders try to stretch their existing vision to be big enough to include everyone.

We...

- Take an existing financial measure and multiply it by 100.

- Share a prophetic dream about the future of the business.

- Post it in big, shiny letters on the wall.

This is a mistake, though. We hand down the story, but it's really a story about the past, not a picture of the future.

As I became a Renegade-Leader, I had to make what I call "The Destination Shift." It was more important than ever for my team and me to be compelled to do our best work and stay united in going the same direction toward our ultimate vision.

"Depend on the rabbit's foot if you will, but remember it didn't work for the rabbit." – R.E. Shay

SHIFT **# 4**

THE WORLD SAYS

~~"Grind and you might get lucky."~~

BUT YOU SAID

~~"I'll make my own luck."~~

THE *Destination*

SAYS *Start with*

SHIFT

# the END in mind.

## THE DESTINATION SHIFT

~~Shift #4: "Grind, and you might get lucky."~~
~~"I'll make my own luck."~~
Start with the end in mind.

I was consulting with a senior leadership team a few years back, and in one particular meeting we started talking about where they were aiming to go as a business in the next several years.

When I have these conversations about long-term vision with teams, most struggle to get their vision or target out of their head and onto paper in a concise, shareable format.

But not this team.

It took them no time to name where they were headed and even more miraculously, they were completely aligned. Everyone had the same answer. They all said, "we are going to be a 100-million-dollar company in three years."

Most senior leadership teams would love to have that much clarity and unity, and it would certainly make my job easier! But there was a problem.

I said, "OK, that's great; you know WHERE you're headed, and you know WHEN you want to get there, but we're missing one thing."

They looked confused.

"It's not enough to know where you're going and when," I responded. "We need to know WHY."

The more we unpacked this thought, the more we all realized that what sounded compelling and clear to them was murkier than what they thought. Right away, the reasons they could share for this goal all came back to reaching an exit and walking away as the primary shareholders with their checks. There's nothing wrong with that being the target for the people sitting around that table. The problem was it had nothing to do with the 60 employees or the 100s of customers they served. Their WHY was too small to carry the power of a common purpose.

Daniel Coyle, in his book *The Culture Code,* explains this with such clarity. He says highly-successful teams have three qualities in common:

**1.** Belonging

**2.** Vulnerability

**3.** Common Purpose

*Common purpose* tells us: WHY we are going where we're going, WHY we push forward when it's tough, WHY we're all here together, and WHY where we want to go matters.

An audacious goal becomes a compelling destination for our organization when it tells us WHERE we're going, WHEN we plan to get there, WHY it matters, and WHY we matter in the journey.

This concept should unite shareholders and employees, and possibly even customers. It should give us a sense of belonging in a vision that is greater than what we can do on our own.

There's no better example I can give you of this kind of literal groundbreaking purpose and compelling destination than the leaders System & Soul serves at The Academy of Warren.

## TAKE IT FROM A RENEGADE (AND THEIR COACH)

### Amy Watts
Office Manager,
Academy of Warren

### Bill Green
System &
Soul Coach

*If you'd told Amy Watts three years ago that the old, abandoned grocery store on 8 Mile Road in her hometown of Warren, Michigan, was going to be a school for 800 students and her biggest problem would be figuring out how she could get a fleet of buses organized so even more kids from the neighborhood could attend, she wouldn't have believed you.*

*"It wasn't… um…a 'traditional' school" she said. "No windows, very dark, but our Chief Academic Officer, Mr. Oronde Kearney, came with his vision. People loved it, and in such a short time, they transformed the school."*

*"Right outside my office window we have a gardening area now. We have skylights in every hallway, big glass windows for the students to look outside their classrooms, and lots of outdoor learning space with picnic tables and bean bag chairs where they can come sit and read or play games. It's just a total 360; I wish everyone could see it."*

*Their System & Soul Coach, Bill Green, recalls his first impression of the place when he started working with their leadership team. "Lining the halls of the school are historic photos of the building's history in the community. Each wall is filled with hand-painted art celebrating African-American culture—many of the pieces crafted by the school's staff members. The "soul" of the school comes alive everywhere you look."*

*Over the last several years, the school has transformed, not only the 100,000 square foot property into an incredible place for hundreds of students and their families, but in the way they operate as they expand.*

*"Like many other schools, the Academy of Warren has a strategic plan." Bill said. "It contains in-depth detail on topics like curriculum, funding, food service, safety, building maintenance, and the like. What the team realized, though, as we've worked together, is that they were not as prepared to execute that plan without a system that enabled them to gain clarity on their core purpose and take control of the day-to-day challenges that derailed them.*

*So, in my initial work with the school, we spent two full days together defining their identity, clarifying their core purpose, describing the culture they aspired to, and placing "bets" for the school's future goals.*

*Their destination is now being displayed at various spots throughout the school's hallways to remind the students and staff of their commitment to executing their vision.*

*"We are the only K-8 Academy in Macomb County that offers a lifelong educational experience in a safe, secure, and state of the art environment. We are going to be in the top 20% of all the schools in Macomb County by 2030 because the health of a society depends upon producing quality individuals."*

*"I told Bill in our last leadership team meeting," Amy continues, "that before when we came to work our goal was to help the kids get the education they need, but now it's more than that. We set a mission and a goal, and now it's like we just operate with more purpose. Our team is in sync and people are accountable and we're able to bring more of the ideas and initiatives we dream up to fruition."*

Daniel Coyle says it this way, "[Building purpose is...] not as simple as carving a mission statement in granite or encouraging everyone to recite a hymnal of catchphrases. It's a never-ending process of trying, failing, reflecting and, above all, learning. High-purpose environments don't descend on groups from on high; they are dug out of the ground, over and over, as a group navigates its problems together and evolves to meet the challenges of a fast-changing world."

A compelling destination makes the grind worth it and the luck irrelevant. More importantly, it makes it worth going on the journey together.

**YOUR TURN:**

So often when we set goals for our teams to drive toward, they lack the power and clarity we envision them having. Here's a simple formula to create a compelling destination for your organization:

## Fill in the blanks:

**We are going to do/be/go**

[ *where you're going* ]

**by**

[ *when* ]

**because**

[ *why it matters* ]

Now, for the practical stuff:

- ● Name the measurable (where) and project a realistic outcome and tangible milestone.

- ● Work as a leadership team to name what we really want for this business.

- ● Ensure everyone in the organization knows it and knows our progress toward it.

- ● Track it on a weekly, monthly, or quarterly basis.

This is how you not only set a Destination, but how you make progress toward it as a team.

WHERE = The long term goal. Our driving vision.

WHEN = The realistic time frame we plan to get there. This sets pace more than anything.

WHY = The reasons that sustain us and include every person on the team.

We are the only K-8 Academy in Macomb County that offers a lifelong educational experience in a safe, secure, and state of the art environment.

We are going to be in the top 20% of all schools in Macomb County by 2030, because the health of a society depends upon producing quality individuals.

# Chapter 5

# THE BIG SIX

## SHIFT #5: THE ETHOS SHIFT

*Great spirits have always encountered violent opposition
from mediocre minds. The mediocre mind is incapable
of understanding the man who refuses to bow blindly to
conventional prejudices and chooses instead to express his
opinions courageously and honestly.* —Albert Einstein

Very early in the growth of my marketing agency, I got an unheard
of opportunity to work with one of the largest brands in the
world. My small, struggling shop was microscopic compared
to this company and the competition we beat. It was a huge
victory and it came with an even better paycheck. At first, I felt
as though I'd struck gold and the dark days of wringing my
hands over cash flow and closing new clients were behind us.

But there was a problem.

Every time I showed up to meet with this big, awesome
company at this big, amazing office to present my work to a
big, impressive conference room, and collect my big, beautiful
check, all I could see were zombies. I got zombie feedback.

And zombie projects to work on. And delivered my team's work to a room full of dead-eyed executives. Their expectations were so mediocre that it started to feel like the hours of work we had put into these projects didn't really matter.

Over time I genuinely dreaded working with them. I wondered how these zombies were still employed. Their apathy and obvious disinterest in doing unique work was soul-crushing for a Renegade like me.

And even worse, they kept asking for more work.

I couldn't imagine watching my business get absorbed into this mammoth-zombie company. I also didn't start a business to work with people who wanted me to play their game, check boxes, and conform to their system.

So I turned them down and went back to scraping along.

Any other agency owner in my vicinity would have thought I'd just given up my golden ticket. I did too for a while, but it was honestly the best decision I could have made because it wasn't who I was.

Giving in wasn't an option because it violated everything I valued: authenticity, quality, curiosity.

We are programmed as human beings to find ways to conform in order to fit in and survive in our society. The more sameness there is, the greater chance we give ourselves to be accepted and "make it." Which is why the trademark trait of any Renegade—their unwillingness to conform—is so radical and seemingly dangerous.

Bucking traditions, whether it be a hairstyle no one else has or a starting the business no one else would dare to endeavor, the Renegade has a drive to do what they are told not to and what everyone else avoids. It can end up looking like rebellion for rebellion's sake but, really, it's the Renegade's own set of principles in play.

- Peter Pan refused to grow up.

- Ferris Bueller refused to adhere to the system.

- Tommy Boy and Richard refused to change who they were to act like "proper" business people.

Renegades know that when they start playing their *OWN* game, possibility thrives and they live more closely aligned with the *Truest* version of who they are.

They never have, and never would, want to be normal or status quo because normal is boring. Nobody remembers normal. Normal is short-changing potential. Making much effort to be normal as a person or as a brand is a very good way to get lost in the crowd.

When we aim for normal, we diminish our uniqueness and inherent creativity. We don't show up and start any conversations. And we definitely don't spark any interest.

Maybe, worst of all—and I see this all the time in businesses I've worked with—they don't get who or what they really want because they're too afraid to really claim who they really are.

Renegades play their own game based on the values
they're willing to sacrifice for, and the unshakable
belief that the authentic power of their business is
in staying true to who they are above all else.

**Tommy Boy:** *"We don't take no prisoners."*

**Richard:** *"We don't take no for an answer."*

## THE SHIFT
As a Renegade, you're thinking, "No shit, dude.
That's why I started my own thing. I gotta do me."

I'm with you. Likely the brand you've built and the internal
culture you've created in your business looks a lot like…well,
you. Your personality, your style, your values. The problem is,
the identity of a growing business has to be bigger than the
founder. If it's all you, then there's no room for anyone else.

That's what we have to overcome as we shift the ethos
and identity of our business from "me" to "we."

The business today is not just about you being you—your
personality and style. It's about *us.* The *ethos* of our
business is a collective decision about who
we are and how we do business together.

SHIFT # 5

THE WORLD SAYS

~~Don't make a scene.~~

BUT YOU SAID

~~"I gotta do me."~~

THE Ethos

SAYS We gotta

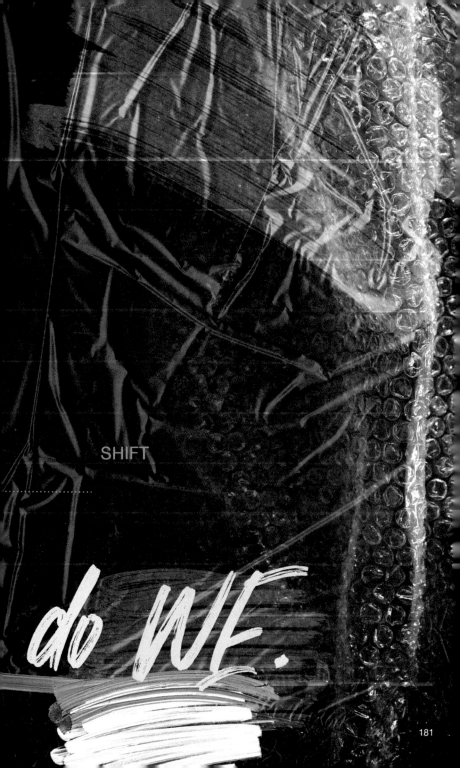

SHIFT

do WE.

## THE ETHOS SHIFT

~~Shift #5: Don't make a scene.~~
~~"I gotta do me."~~
We gotta do we.

A firmly defined ethos tells us who we are as a team, what matters to us, and how we will work together. Our ethos embodies the shared purpose we have in the work we do and a shared identity that carries the pride of our unique mission.

As a Renegade this all makes sense to you and comes naturally. You have no doubt about who you are, you're not afraid to rock the boat or stand out from the crowd. That confidence has likely been part of the reason your team, clients and customers are attracted to you and your business.

Your role as you shift to a Renegade-Leader is to help everyone else in your organization see that...

*Fitting in is driven by Fear.*
*Standing out is driven by Purpose.*

The challenge is inviting the team into the conversation around who you are and want to be as an organization, and then giving them the confidence to pick up the flag and move together knowing what you're all about.

Remember the movie, Braveheart? William Wallace (Mel Gibson) rides across the front lines of his army shouting a moving and unforgettable speech. If you went back and watched that famous scene, you would notice flag bearers scattered through the ranks. Now, I'll be honest, the flag bearer in any medieval army would not be a role I would personally sign up for. This person marches first into the battle with only a flag between them and the enemy—no spear, or sword, or bow. But really, when you think about it, it's one of the most important roles in the entire infantry. The flag bearer was essential to guide the army forward and to know when to retreat.

It's not about having a flag for the sake of the flag. It's a reminder of our collective identity. It reminds us what we fight for.

If we can build the business around who we are collectively, what we value as a whole, and what we're exceptional at doing with our combined skills, the outer expression to our market becomes shockingly attractive to the people we want to do business with.

I've found three simple ways to start thinking about and aligning the work we do to an ethos that stands out and builds confidence within the team. Remember, your job now is not to sprint ahead and do these things on your own. You're shaping who you are, together.

### 1. Have the guts. Be the only.

If your business was the only company in the world doing or delivering on one promise, what would it be?

It's an intimidating question and seemingly impractical, but if you can be clear on what breaks the mold in your industry, you will dial in on who you attract and create champions for upholding what you do internally.

# HAVE THE GUTS TO BE THE only

# make it HURT.

## 2. Make it hurt.

Your ethos is founded in the values you uphold together. Not your values. Not the values of some company you admire. The values that are real and true to your team. I love how Patrick Lencioni says this:

*"Indeed, an organization considering a values initiative must first come to terms with the fact that, when properly practiced, values inflict pain. They make some employees feel like outcasts. They limit an organization's strategic and operational freedom and constrain the behavior of its people. They leave executives open to heavy criticism for even minor violations. And they demand constant vigilance."*

Your values don't just need to be "core," they need to be real. Your values should drive decisions in your business about who you work with, who you hire, how you handle opportunities, and every challenge that comes up. You should hire people based on your values. You should have hard conversations based on your values. You should reward and recognize values when they show up.

# DO *one* THING

### 3. Do one thing.

There's a fable Jim Collins made famous about a hedgehog and a fox in his book, *Good to Great*. As the story goes, there was a fox who tried to think of a new and clever way to eat a hedgehog every day, and every time the fox tried to come after her, the hedgehog curled up in a ball to protect herself.

The moral of the story is: the fox knows many things. But the hedgehog knows one thing.

Your role as a Renegade-Leader is to help your business find their hedgehog. Your tendency will be to act like the fox, but your organization needs to know one thing they can do over and over to create a defensible and scalable business.

When they can do that, they will find their authentic, organizational power. That power comes from knowing three key components: what you love, what you're the best in the world at, and what drives your economic engine.

Usually, the people who get it, who get you, are a smaller crowd than the entire market that exists - unless you are an accountant or running a funeral home - it's hard to say that everyone is really your potential customer. People get scared by this. They think, "Well if we're too different, if we're too unique or too niche, we'll drive away perfectly good business."

Keep in mind, if you aren't willing to polarize anyone, you likely won't be very attractive either. A magnet can only attract with a power equal to its power to repel.

Marketing and branding expert, Al Ries, says in his book
*Positioning,* it's much more powerful to own a small
category than to be a small player in a big category.

That goes for who you attract internally
and it bleeds out externally.

In the marketing agency I started almost two decades
ago, I came in with a very clear and confident
idea of the values I wanted to uphold.

> **Love:** We put others before ourselves.

> **Create:** We find the unseen solution.

> **Steward:** We do more with less.

> **Engage:** We understand, deliver, and drive.

Since then, the values have changed and changed again.
I want you to hear what that's looked like for me and my
business, not because I think I got it right the first time or
to tip my own hat. I want to show you what amazes me
about values that transcend individual people, and I want
you to hear it from a Renegade-Leader who gets this
better than me, and maybe better than anyone I know.

## TAKE IT FROM A RENEGADE:

*Kate Neri*

CEO, Syrup Marketing

*I started working for Benj eight years ago as an account lead at Syrup Marketing. Before then, I'd worked in a big corporate environment, so coming to this small agency I expected it to feel different, but the minute I walked in the office for my interview, I could tell something was different in a way I never would have expected.*

*It started with the way the team acted in the interviews I had, and it continued as I took the job and started to see how the business ran day-by-day.*

*People were unusually calm and understanding when mistakes were made. There was a "got your back" approach to failures where I expected reprimands and punishment.*

*Everyone really, genuinely cared about the work they were doing for the clients—like all of them, all the time.*

*People were present and focused during office hours, and they actually shut it off and had full lives outside of work. And back then, especially in the agency world, that was not the norm.*

*And maybe best of all, Benj, the guy with the most on his plate, was usually the first to pull the Spikeball net out of the closet and interrupt the work day for a couple of games to help everyone re-energize.*

*It was the first time I'd ever experienced a company that cared about me as a whole person, and cared so deeply about doing exceptional work for the businesses we served, while also never taking ourselves too seriously.*

*It wasn't just that it was fun and friendly, it was much deeper than that. I could tell that everyone on our little team understood and lived the values of our business. And Benj definitely led the way.*

*We reached a point three or four years ago where I watched Benj discover that if he kept leading the organization the way he was, we wouldn't be able to scale to the size and team we have now. It had to have taken so much thought and trust in our team to step back like he did. I was seriously in awe of him for making that decision. It was absolutely the right thing. And not because the values and the tone he set for the team were limiting, that wasn't really it. He just knew that there needed to be more space for diverse voices at the table to be competitive and expand the way we dreamed we would.*

*He took a huge step back and, for a couple of years, our team reinvented some of the ethos he'd built the business on.*

*Over the years that followed, it wasn't what changed drastically that was so amazing about our business. It was actually what stayed constant as the team doubled in size. We experienced a pandemic, and we totally reworked the market we served. The constant was the values and what we stood for as a team.*

*Fast forward to now, and I'm the CEO of Syrup.*

*The values we had when I started as an account lead are the values I lead our team through today. The words are the same, but the definitions changed. At one time the values we lived out looked a lot like Benj and even some of the people who started the business from the beginning. But they expanded to include everyone—to become values that resonated with each person, in each role on the team.*

*It wasn't a revolution, it was an evolution.*

*I think that was possible because the values have always been the company's, not just Benj or any one person. They really belonged to the team.*

*Now, we hold the same values, but by their definitions we're able to include everyone and every role more fully.*

**Love**
We bring out the best in each other through genuine respect and honesty.

**Create**
We are resourceful problem solvers.

**Steward**
We responsibly use all our talents, time and resources to serve.

**Engage**
We are dialed in and take full ownership of our work.

Now I see this evolution in the work we do branding and marketing for clients. We come face to face with these moments of courage and trust the Founder has to recognize to really build a lasting and "big enough" identity for their business. We have to help them see what we had to learn, and what Benj demonstrated for us years ago, to go forward as a team with the courage to be driven by our purpose and values, knowing that we won't be "for" everyone, but we will create a space for the people who belong and propel us forward.

**YOUR TURN:**

- **Consider what values belong to your business.**
  Make a list of what matters most to your organization
  as you make major decisions: business deals,
  hiring/firing, rewarding, and recognizing.

- **Write your Onliness Statement**—get clear about what
  makes your business unique—and rally your team.

- **Create your Hedgehog**—clarify the authentic
  power your business holds.

p.s. *Remember:* Like a magnet,
our business can only *attract* to the
same level that it is willing to *repel.*

# THE BIG SIX

## SHIFT #6: THE PEOPLE SHIFT

*Don't let others define you. Define yourself."*
Ginni Rometty, Chairman and CEO, IBM

For the first few years of our marriage, my wife Erica was the assistant volleyball coach for Auburn University. She'd played as a division one athlete and basically landed a dream job right out of college, so without question, we moved over 700 miles away from Ohio, where we'd lived most of our lives, to Auburn, Alabama. We knew no one. Her job was the only income we had between the two of us. As you can imagine, we weren't making a lot of money at that time. We bought a townhouse for $69,000 and survived mainly on buffet salad and pizza in the college cafeteria using Erica's staff meal plan.

It was also, of course, an amazing and overwhelmingly cool job. She was one of only a handful of people year over year who got hired for this role in the extremely competitive world of division one sports. She was doing what she loved the most in the highest-performance environment you could ask for. I was so happy for her and, if you know Erica, you would know she was committed to competing and crushing the job 150%.

In Erica's experience, and for most Renegades in the pursuit of something risky and challenging, you're warned by the people who love you and worry about you, "don't quit your day job." What they don't realize is that a day job sounds like death. We'd so much rather be poor, and pursue a dream on our own than on someone else's payroll.

For us, when the dream gets hard, the money runs out, the market dries up, the prototype fails, or the customers can't be found, the impulse is not to pack our bags and start filling out applications on job sites for a proper day job. We push it one step further. This is where our self-sufficiency becomes a superpower. We know that if we keep searching, keep trying, keep moving, and if we can pull ourselves together and push through the parts that suck, we will find our own way.

Renegades know there is no one coming behind them to solve the problem. They don't run into the fight hoping to be rescued. They learn that going their own way means finding their own way. **Self-determination is just a necessity to freedom.**

It was a few months of Erica working in the role before I noticed an unsettling shift. She started coming home anxious and clearly deflated about her work. I would ask her about her day and she would rehash how the head coach shot down her ideas and dismissed her authority again and again. We repeated this routine more and more frequently as time went on, so much so, I was seeing her demeanor about her work change and even worse her confidence in herself. She was getting increasingly more nervous to speak up and voice her ideas. She started doubting her knowledge and ability. And really started to believe she wasn't good enough to do this job. That voice got really loud for her to the point we decided this job wasn't the right fit for her anymore. It was never how we thought that experience would go and the effects of that coach's bad leadership lingered with her for a long time.

I really hated that experience for her and worried that what this coach was saying to her would make her consider ending her career doing what she loved. The thing is, Erica is a Renegade, so quitting is never really an option.

Erica has been saying this mantra for the 23 years we've been married:

**Dream, believe, become.**

> **Dream**—Consider the possibilities.

> **Believe**—Decide and trust you can get there with the right work.

> **Become**—Do the work.

A few years ago she added a 4th word:

*Dream, believe, become, be*

It's a brilliant reminder that sometimes the season we're in is just one of being. Not preparing. Not dreaming. Not deciding. Not becoming. Stepping into the arena as you are right now.

In the last few years I've gotten to watch her "be" in her element, again. Erica was hired to coach for one of the top high school volleyball programs in Georgia. She's already taken her team to the state championship and named Coach of the Year.

I love that she took the leap to begin with. And I love, even more, that she picked up her dream again. What I love the most, though, is that she wins and shines not because she alone is a tenacious Renegade, but because she's taught a team of young women how to capture and carry that Renegade spirit together.

## THE SHIFT

Maybe, the most challenging of all the shifts we have to make as Renegade-Founders is moving from one, to 10, to 100. And I don't mean scaling revenues or earning market share.

I mean the people—everyone from our business partners, to the assistant who keeps us in line, to the UPS delivery guy that helps ship our product. We not only create a new economy when we build a business, but we also create an ecosystem, a society, a community, and, most definitely, a culture.

We have the ability and privilege to give dignity to the people who work next to us, and the multitudes of people their lives touch, too.

This is our toughest challenge as we move from Renegade-Founder to Renegade-Leader because we've usually been looking at people in our business in the wrong way.

**Choose your own adventure:**

Some Renegades see the team and the people as....

| | |
|---|---|
| A huge source of fulfillment and joy. High on the adventure. *100% relationship.* | A liability or asset to the thing they created. A means to an end. *100% object.* |

When they started building their teams, they both had great hopes and intentions for what it would become, but they never thought it would end up....

# A Playground
## Masquerading as a Business

**Our mission statement:**
We're in the people business, so don't ask about numbers, goals, or process improvements.

**Our company values:**
- Pizza Fridays
- Taco Tuesdays
- Ice cream Mondays
- Brews and Board Meetings
- Perks, perks, perks!
- Fun, fun, fun!

**Benefits to team include:**
- Free lunch
- Long meetings with no purpose
- Wasted resources
- Lacking competition
- Being hopelessly confused about what you're contributing to

# A Dystopian Hellscape

## Masquerading as a Business

**Our mission statement:**
Eat, sleep and breathe this place, and
remember, if you don't, you're replaceable.

**Our company values:**
- Efficiency
- Hard work
- Process makes perfect
- There's a protocol for that
- We're here to sell widgets,
  not make friends.

**Benefits to team include:**
- Feeling like a cog in a machine
- Suppressed ideas and feelings
- Burn out
- General sense of dread
- Being hopelessly confused about
  what you're contributing to

Either way, we end up in the same place: **Soul-sick.**

The playground entertains anyone who wants to
join. It's fun and exciting. People are happy. But the
soul becomes cheap; it loses its meaning when the
people and culture don't create value out of it.

The hellscape can produce nothing because it has no value.
It severs a business from its humanity. It's cold, mechanical,
and numb. The soul atrophies and dies out. People are starved
for meaning and knowing how they matter in the big picture.

SHIFT # 6

THE WORLD SAYS

~~"It matters who you work for."~~

BUT YOU SAID

~~"I work for myself."~~

THE

*People*

SAYS

## We work

SHIFT

TOGETHER.

## THE PEOPLE SHIFT

Shift #6: "It matters who you work for."
"I work for myself."
We work together.

A few years ago, I was watching a documentary called, *The Pursuit.* Economist Arthur Brooks is standing in the middle of a crowded, muddy street in Chennai, India. It's not a modern city. In fact, the place in the scene is very old, eclectic, maybe even a little run down. Crates and boxes, clay pots, and textiles are stacked randomly all along the street. Brooks navigates a narrow path between buildings and, as he walks, he talks about how he's visited this city occasionally for the last 20 years of his life and these visits have led him to a profound realization:

"They are us, separated by time."

He goes on to explain that Chennai, like the rest of India, has risen out of poverty over the last 20 years as government systems changed and commerce was democratized. All those boxes, clay pots, and textiles filling the street around him are signs of a new economy.

That scene has always stuck with me. It taps a nerve. "They are us, separated by time." Me. You. The guy on your street who runs an IT services business out of his garage.

There's this overwhelming sense of victory to watch people discover the value they can create in the world, and stake their claim.

I tend to think about the individuals they zoom in on during that scene in Chennai, and my heart swells because over the next 20 years the one will become 10, will become 100, will become 1,000.

# THE culture IS NOT YOURS TO control.

**A Renegade is a world-altering ripple effect.**

There are three counterintuitive ideas I've come to believe and practice as I've led people in my organizations:

**1.** The culture is not yours to fix.

**2.** The problems are not yours to solve.

**3.** The people are not yours to lead.

### The Culture Is Not Yours To Control

The culture you create is an outcome of how the people in your organization keep and live out the values consistently. It's the result of consistent, habitual action that your organization reinforces.

You can't fix your culture by waving your wand or dictating "how things will be from now on" because whatever you're trying to accomplish requires an army. You need dedication. You need follow-through. They need to be inspired and deeply in touch with the meaning behind why we do what we do to stay continuously in step. They have to want this vision for the culture to be true. **The culture belongs to the** *Team*

Intentionally or unintentionally, the culture is built on the repeated behavior of the people in the organization. We often overlook these normalized routines and may even assume it's standard practice for businesses everywhere.

- Answering emails at midnight and on weekends

- Leaving it up to one person every day to make the coffee

- Rewarding great work with thoughtful, meaningful gifts

These behaviors can just happen, they can wear down our culture, or they can be engineered to happen in the way that helps us be more of who we really aspire to be.

It's one thing to say we want to be the kind of place that is _____.

But it doesn't happen without intentional action.

At System & Soul, we call this engineering culture.

**Values** (standard we believe in)
+
**Organizational Habits** (the things we do together)
=
**Culture** (the attributes we want to be true).

Habits build toward culture, but habits can't be carried by one or two highly disciplined, responsible individuals. They must be organizational, agreed to, accounted for, scheduled, resourced, and bonded with our collective values.

### The Problems Are Not Yours To Solve

The inevitable problems of the business stay your problems if they're always up to you to solve. Most people don't make decisions because they haven't been empowered to do so … or worse, after they do, we swoop in and want it done "our way." We're better off teaching our people to think like owners and solve their own problems in any role than to hoard responsibility. The people closest to the problems should be equipped to solve them and have a degree of autonomy that enables them to move forward with resolution.

THE ~~problems~~ ARE ~~NOT YOURS~~ TO ~~solve.~~

One of the most rewarding and jarring moments we experience as Renegade-Leaders is the moment in conversations when you no longer need to speak up first to resolve a challenge. Your silence and their excitement to jump in, bring their ideas, and collaborate together to solve the problem at hand is a good sign, but it feels incredibly awkward.

What I've learned, and I teach the Renegades I work with now, is this:

1. Teach them how to take the problem to the right people. When teams and roles are incredibly clear, then they are equipped with a structure not only for the people in the business but also a structure that shows them where their problem belongs. As always, talk TO the person, not ABOUT the person.

2. Give them a cadence and a framework for finding solutions. To help them become great problem solvers, we can provide them with a pattern to follow and analyze the situation before them. Give them a weekly meeting, at the same time, same place, with the same agenda and same formula for discussing and taking action on urgent and significant opportunities. (I'll share a tool I use at the end of this chapter.)

3. Create space for them to think. If you're quick and decisive like most Renegades I know, it can be agonizing to wait for others to catch up to the solutions you had in mind hours or days earlier than they seem to be able to find them. If we want them to catch up though, they need a chance to work those muscles more and build that endurance. As they grow in their autonomy and ability to problem solve, I empower teams with a tool called 1-3-1. For the one problem you have, before you bring it to me to discuss, make sure you can clearly state the problem, consider three potential solutions, and bring a recommendation for which one you are leaning toward.

# THE people ARE ~~NOT YOURS~~ TO *lead.*

## The People Are Not Yours To Lead

The people can never really be led by you. They can be managed by you and follow what you do, but leadership is ultimately their call. Leadership is who we are and how we demonstrate care for the people we lead.

Remember earlier we talked about becoming inwardly sound and others focused? You can't do that for them. Our role is to be an example in how we lead ourselves and become increasingly secure, settled, self-aware, empathic, and loving. This kind of leading is far more contagious, pervasive, and sustainable for you and for them. They will watch you and notice. They will see how you approach uncertainties, upsets, and difficulties, and when you show up as a leader, they will understand more of what leadership requires from them.

As we live this out ourselves, we can demonstrate care and be a source of insight for them in how we give them feedback along the way.

My friend and fellow Renegade-Leader, Michael Allosso, coined this as "T.S.P.," Truthful, Specific, Positive feedback. Michael is an actor, consultant, and director for many stage performances, and in all environments he leads, he uses this concept. For the performances he directs, Michael says he's aware that the performing cast has 14 rehearsals before their opening show. For each of those 14 rehearsals it's absolutely imperative that he gives each person on stage the truthful, specific, positive feedback they need to perform better in the next rehearsal.

Imagine addressing the people we lead with that kind of imperative. The curtain goes up on the players on your team on opening night. It is up to them to learn their lines and know their part. But are you giving them the feedback to really step into their potential?

Your incredible responsibility and privilege is to help them better know who they are, what they really want, and what they are capable of.

There are six simple questions that I think allow us to unpack a lot of this with our teams as we encourage and challenge them in their leadership. I use these during quarterly meetings, as well as in one-on-one sessions with team members. These questions address what System & Soul Coach Jonathan King has coined as the Six Dimensions of Compensation.

1. **Emotional Compensation**: Do you enjoy your work?

2. **Social Compensation:** Do you like the people you work with?

3. **Psychological Compensation:** Are you learning and growing in your career?

4. **Spiritual Compensation:** Does your work have meaning and purpose?

5. **Physical Compensation:** Does your work give you the margin and flexibility you want?

6. **Financial Compensation:** Are you appropriately compensated for your work?

The People Shift is a decision to invite your people to step into the ring with you. Invite them to give their own words and dreams to the story the business tells. Invite them to think about it as if it's theirs. Trust that the right people will say yes.

**Take the 6 Dimensions of Compensation assessment here:**

**TAKE IT FROM A RENEGADE:** *Billy Pierce*
President and CEO, Dalton PHC

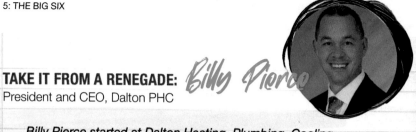

*Billy Pierce started at Dalton Heating, Plumbing, Cooling and Electric in 2015 as an HVAC Manager and bought the company in 2021. At that time he knew he wanted to share his vision and instill values in the business but he was asking himself, "how do I execute that? How do I turn that vision from just something I see into reality? How do I communicate that? All these ideas lived in my head and I realized it can't be that way. As the business was growing, I wanted the people growing with it. I wanted them to feel empowered, like they loved coming to work, like they had clarity around their position."*

*He also knew he needed to do it ASAP. "I didn't want it to be a 15-year journey to get from one out of ten to seven out of ten. I wanted to get to a ten out of ten and stay at a ten out of ten."*

*He realized that in order to get there he had to start with how he was leading his team and showing up for them. "I'm a strategy person. I'm not necessarily people oriented. I'm task oriented. So I could sit in my office and think all day, but of course I would get interrupted. It used to bother me, but now I understand that it affects people out there. And what I really wanted was good morale. I wanted them to know, I really care about you and I'm there for you."*

*So, as Billy and his team worked with System & Soul Coach Bill Green to build out their values and decided on the habits that would drive the culture, they came up with an unorthodox solution.*

*"One of our core values is 'your problem is my problem.'
We invite the team to interrupt us in meetings if they really
need help because I received feedback that they felt
they couldn't get to leadership and management to solve
problems effectively because we are always in meetings."*

*And of course that's probably different from how a lot of
people handle it, but we don't want to be like the norm.
We want to be different. We want to do what makes our
people feel like we care and they are a part of the culture."*

*Because of this change in habit, Billy and his
leadership team are more aware than ever of the
challenges that affect the work their team is doing,
and it has revealed untapped methods for strategically
solving problems and growing their business.*

*"I've been filled with more knowledge about what's actually
happening out there on a day-to-day basis. So now I
can take that into consideration and create a strategy
to work around that or fix it for the team as a whole.*

*My dream is that it doesn't depend on me. You know,
do I want to help impact it? Absolutely. I love the fact
that our operator is operating things, and you know, is
a perfect teammate to me. I love that other people are
able to step in and use their strengths to help me and
my weaknesses and my strengths to help them in their
weaknesses. I am a big idea guy. I dream about a lot
of things. I do see the future. I set the tempo for our
culture. But more and more, my goal is to get the culture
I see for us off the walls and into every individual."*

You can't fix it or shape it alone because it's not just yours anymore. **The business belongs to the** *Team* It will either begin to look like their collective effort, passion, gifts, and shared values, or it will look like their dissent and disengagement. What we must learn to master is first how we lead ourselves, how we value others, and then help them discover their part in the story.

*Leadership is not about building your own little kingdom, but about making the world better for those around you. But no one needs you to be their hero. Instead, inspire others to be the heroes of their own lives.*
—Liz Bohannon, Founder and CEO, Sseko

**YOUR TURN:**
When the conversation requires vulnerability, I tell the leaders I work with to go first. When the conversation requires ideas, opinions, or problem-solving, go last.

I want to ask you to go first. Find out how your team is experiencing your leadership right now. Gain an understanding of how they experience you and commit to leading yourself better based on the feedback they're willing to give.

Get a pulse on your
leadership with this
360 assessment:

6:: The

Chapter 6

# THE PARADOX

I thought it fitting to leave you with an idea from a Renegade whose impact started in my life in 1989. Maybe you know him.

Mr. Keating, aka "Captain" aka Robin Williams in the movie *Dead Poets Society*, shows up at the start of senior year for a group of polished, elite prep school boys whose greatest ambitions appear to be rooted solely in the school's expectations and what their parents have already determined for them.

Mr. Keating is the school's newly hired English teacher, and on his first day, he asks a student in his class to read aloud the preface to their poetry textbook.

The preface states how poetry is a formula, based on answering two questions: one about the importance of the subject, and the other about the perfection of the form. "Once these two questions have been answered, the poem's greatness becomes a relatively simple matter."

Keating goes along with this and draws a graph on the board. He writes an equation for the way a great poem is

# "EXCREMENT"

determined in the textbook. And then, he turns around
to face the class and says,

## "Excrement."

The formula, the prescription, the thoughtless, lifeless
system is crap.

If you know the story, Mr. Keating goes on to simultaneously
inspire those languishing students and buck the entire
system they exist in—of course, pissing off a lot of
people who thrive in the system along the way.

He teaches his students to "suck the marrow out of life" but
avoid "choking on the bone." He is full of soul: an inviting guide,
curious, somewhat unpredictable, but consistently caring. And
even though he breaks the rules, he honors the truth in the
traditions and universal values he's teaching them through poetry.
Those who see the value in what he clearly and completely
loves are drawn to him. Those who don't understand and are
threatened by him do everything they can to oppose him.

Mr. Keating is an inwardly-sound badass.
An incredible Renegade-Leader.

But he wasn't just a Renegade-Leader for ripping pages
out of textbooks and calling them excrement.

He became a true Renegade-Leader when he was
willing to walk away.

Mr. Keating gets fired. The system he exists in has enough of
him rattling the cage. They think he will disappear and become
an uncomfortable blip on the timeline of their institution.

But, it's too late.

As he collects his belongings and exits his classroom for the last time, the students he'd spent all year with call out to him, "O, Captain, my Captain," and stand on their desks. (You should be crying at this point.)
Mr. Keating thanks them and walks away.

**Here's what I'm not saying:** Pack it up, walk away from your business. They are better off without you.

**Here's what I am saying:** You, Renegade, will not lose relevance, importance, or value in this business if you make these choices to evolve and empower. It's not possible because the impact has and will continue to run deep in the organization you've built.

The paradox to embrace is that you will always be a Renegade. You will always be wildly independent, and you can't lose that. You can't. The world needs you to buck its systems, break things, and discover what isn't there yet. And at the same time, cross the Founder Gap into the ranks of Renegade-Leaders.

**Ultimately, the shift to clarity, control, freedom, and dignity in your organization begins with you.**

**Bet with intention.** The dignity of *clarity*

**Set the bassline.** The dignity of *consistency*

**Know when you are winning.** The dignity of *success*

**Start with the end in mind.** The dignity of *why*

**We gotta do we.** The dignity of *identity*

**We work together.** The dignity of *humanity*

These shifts are yours to initiate. These are
the shifts that lead to breakthroughs.

This is how you create dignity that outlasts your individual
conversations, the hours you spend in the business,
your plan for today, for next year, and your lifespan.

You'll know you're on the right track when you're sitting
silently, watching the people around you step in where
you always filled the gap. Their voices are different, their
solutions are not quite yours, but they echo the leadership,
values, destination, purpose, and identity perfectly.

The dignity you give ensures the lifetime
and reach of your business.

You are finding yourself now in a familiar place—the uncertain,
uncomfortable, and unknown. These choices don't always
result in immediate relief; they take time and intention just like
anything worthwhile. You'll doubt yourself. You'll feel like this is
the dumbest decision you could make with the one-of-a-kind
business you built. You'll find that not everyone will be able to
go on the journey with you. Not everyone will understand.

Remember though, this is what you live for.
Charge ahead, see what you discover.
Break rules. Find Freedom.

And Renegade, if you only remember one thing, remember,

*you are a ripple effect*

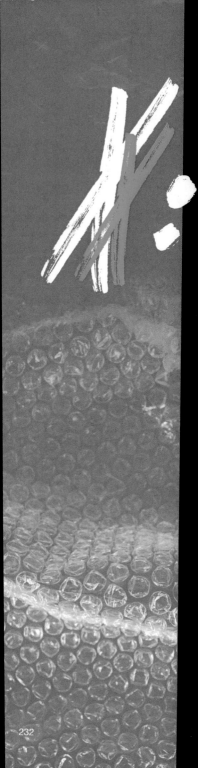

232

# ABOUT THE AUTHORS

## BENJ MILLER

Authenticity, breaking the rules, and creating clarity
are the core of Benj Miller's life and work.

Benj has founded 10 businesses in his 20 years of
entrepreneurial experience and helped coach over 100 brands.
He's driven by the desire to help small businesses make the
greatest possible impact on the communities they serve. He
now dedicates his time to helping other business owners
catalyze growth through the System & Soul Framework
and find game-changing breakthroughs in the process.

He lives in Atlanta, GA with his wife of twenty-
two years and their four amazing kids.

In 2021, Benj partnered with Chris White and McKenzie Reeves
Decker to create System & Soul. A business framework to help
organizations move from founder-led to leadership-team-led
so they can continue to grow, stay accountable, and become
irresistible places for great people to do their best work.

Learn more about Benj and his organization
at SysteamandSoul.com

## CHRIS WHITE

Chris left the comfort of a 9-5 job because he realized he wasn't building anything like his parents or grandparents did with their businesses. He took his entrepreneurial leap of faith over 25 years ago and hasn't looked back!

Having successfully built 6 companies and 3 exits, he now passionately pursues radically candid conversations with a relentless drive to mastery (and plenty of fun along the way) as he coaches clients through the System & Soul Framework. He has helped over 160 companies and hundreds of other coaches gain skills that transform their businesses on the path to breakthrough.

Outside of his coaching practice, he founded The Micro Business Academy, co-founded System & Soul, and hosted the System & Soul Podcast. Additionally he co-founded the EOS® software, Ninety.io, and co-authored *The Clarity Field Guide*.

He lives in Orlando, Florida with his incredible wife, Darlene, and their lovable lab, Buddy.

## MCKENZIE REEVES DECKER

McKenzie started working at 13 cleaning tables and restocking condiments at her dad's Chick-Fil-A restaurant. From early on she learned to value operational excellence with a focus on serving the customer above all else.

This drive for industry excellence and servant leadership led her to work with North Point Ministries and later Maxwell Leadership as a division director. Outside of her day-to-day leadership roles, she also pursued a graduate degree in creative writing and in 2019 received a Masters in Fine Arts.

In 2020, she joined Benj Miller and Chris White as a business partner, Operator, and content writer. Since then, She co-founded System & Soul, co-authored the *Clarity Field Guide*, *Renegades*, and has been a contributor on the *System & Soul* Podcast. Her passion and purpose is to fill the gaps, be a leader others want to follow, and help others craft their remarkable stories.

Outside of her work, McKenzie spends her time cooking, gardening, hiking with her husband Jake, and playing a ridiculous amount of fetch with their dog, Sable.

# REFERENCES

Arvind, Dr. Janani. "Sadhguru's Quotes - Sadhguru's Teachings on Life, Love & Spirituality." *Yeh Hai India,* 19 Apr. 2023, yehaindia. com/sadhgurus-quotes-on-life/#:~:text=%E2%80%9CThe%20 walls%20of%20self%2Dprotection,not%20reveal%20 itself%20to%20you.%E2%80%9D.

Batra, Kadambari Rao. Start-ups and Disruption: Paradigms Built on People, Business and Technology. India, SAGE Publications, 2022.

Bohannon, Liz. "Liz Bohannon: Beginner's Pluck." *Global Leadership Network,* 26 Aug. 2019, globalleadership.org/articles/leading-yourself/liz-bohannon-beginners-pluck/?locale=en.

Brown, Brené. Dare to Lead: Brave Work. Tough Conversations. Whole Hearts.. United States, Random House Publishing Group, 2018.

Carpenter, Shelby. "IBM CEO Ginni Rometty to Women: 'Never Let Someone Define Who You Are.'" *Forbes*, 19 Oct. 2016, www.forbes. com/sites/shelbycarpenter/2016/10/19/ibm-ceo-ginni-rometty-to-women-never-let-someone-define-who-you-are/?sh=75ef57702b9a.

Chalker, Emelia. "Everyone Has a Plan until They Get Punched in the Mouth." *Commit Works,* 23 Mar. 2022, www.commit.works/ everyone-has-a-plan-until-they-get-punched-in-the-mouth/.

Collins, James Charles. Good to Great: Why Some Companies Make the Leap...and Others Don't. United Kingdom, HarperCollins, 2001.

Combs, Julie, et al. Managing Conflict: 50 Strategies for School Leaders. United Kingdom, Eye On Education, 2008.

Cote, Catherine. "4 Entrepreneur Success Stories to Learn from: HBS Online." *Business Insights Blog,* 20 Jan. 2022, online. hbs.edu/blog/post/successful-entrepreneur-stories.

Coyle, Daniel. The Culture Code: The Secrets of Highly Successful Groups. United Kingdom, Random House Publishing Group, 2018.

Decker, McKenzie, Amy Watts. "Interview with Amy Watts."

Decker, McKenzie, Bill Green. "Interview with Bill Green."

Decker, McKenzie, Billy Pierce. "Interview with Billy Pierce."

Decker, McKenzie, et al. "Interview with Chris White."

Decker, McKenzie, David McMillan. "Interview with David McMillan."

Decker, McKenzie, Kate Neri. "Interview with Kate Neri."

Decker, McKenzie, et al. "Interview with Haley Devlin."

Deming, W. Edwards. The Essential Deming: Leadership Principles from the Father of Quality. United States, McGraw Hill LLC, 2012.

Divilly, Pat. Upgrade Your Life: How to Take Back Control and Achieve Your Goals. Germany, Wiley, 2016.

Ferguson, Ronald F., et al. "Developing Positive Young Adults - Lessons From Two Decades of Youthbuild Programs." *MDRC*, May 2015, www.mdrc.org/sites/default/files/ YouthBuild%20Development%20Paper_2015.pdf.

Gergen, Kenneth J.. The Dialogical Challenge of Leadership Development. United States, Information Age Publishing, Incorporated, 2019.

Harvard Business Review. United States, Graduate School of Business Administration, Harvard University., 2002.

Higson, Phil, and Sturgess, Anthony. Uncommon Leadership: How to Build Competitive Advantage by Thinking Differently. United Kingdom, Kogan Page, 2014.

Jericho, Chris, and Stanley, Paul. No Is a Four-Letter Word: How I Failed Spelling But Succeeded in Life. United States, Hachette Books, 2017.

Kane, Libby. "'shark Tank' Investor: 'Entrepreneurs Are the Only People Who Will Work 80 Hours a Week to Avoid Working 40 Hours a Week.'" Business Insider, 13 July 2016, www.businessinsider. com/lori-greiner-shark-tank-entrepreneurs-2016-7.

Labhart, Noah, and Andrew Louder. "S8 Bonus: Andrew Louder, Louder Co." Code Story, Code Story, 17 May 2023.

Ladkin, Donna. Rethinking Leadership: A New Look at Old Questions, Second Edition. Germany, Edward Elgar Publishing, 2020.

Lencioni, Patrick M.. The Five Dysfunctions of a Team: A Leadership Fable, 20th Anniversary Edition. Germany, Wiley, 2010.

Leadership and Self-deception: Getting Out of the Box. N.p., ReadHowYouWant, 2008.

Lily, Jade. "'Never Be Limited by Other People's Limited Imaginations.'-Dr. Mae Jemison." Medium, 31 Jan. 2022, medium.com/be-bold/never-be-limited-by-other-peoples-limited-imaginations-dr-mae-jemison-ff794750635c.

Lustberg, Arch. How to Sell Yourself, Revised Edition: Using Leadership, Likability, and Luck to Succeed. United States, Career Press, 2008.

Mathews, Michael Bart. Time to Get Serious Finding Your Moment of Clarity: Discover Your Power Within. United States, Trafford Publishing, 2019.

Miller, Benj, and Erica Miller. "Interview with Erica Miller."

Miller, Benj, Chris White, et al. "Get People To Choose Your Organization with Jeff Boucher and Jonathan Reynolds." Spotify for Podcasters, Titus Talent Strategies, 18 Oct. 2022.

Miller, Benj, John Richie, et al. "Why Most Leaders Suck with John Richie." Spotify for Podcasters, Titus Talent Strategies, 17 Aug. 2021.

Neal, Judi. Edgewalkers: People and Organizations That Take Risks, Build Bridges, and Break New Ground. United States, ABC-CLIO, 2006.

Papola, John, director. *The Pursuit*.

Raz, Guy, et al. "Dude Perfect: Cory Cotton and Tyler Toney." *How I Built This*, 20 Sept. 2021, www.npr.org/2021/09/16/1038140265/ dude-perfect-cory-cotton-and-tyler-toney.

Roosevelt, Theodore. "Citizenship Within A Republic." Paris, France.

Schulman, Tom. *Dead Poets Society (Motion Picture)*. Performance by Robin Williams.

Segal, Gillian Zoe. "This Self-Made Billionaire Failed the LSAT Twice, Then Sold Fax Machines for 7 Years before Hitting Big-Here's How She Got There." *CNBC Small Business Playbook* , 3 Apr. 2019, www.cnbc.com/2019/04/03/self-made-billionaire-spanx-founder-sara-blakely-sold-fax-machines-before-making-it-big.html.

Spiker, Tim. The Only Leaders Worth* Following: Why Some Leaders Succeed, Others Fail, and How the Quality of Our Lives Hangs in the Balance. N.p., Aperio Company, 2020.

Trout, Jack, and Ries, Al. Positioning: The Battle for Your Mind. United Kingdom, McGraw Hill LLC, 2001.

"Truthful, Specific, Positive Feedback®." *TRUTHFUL, SPECIFIC, POSITIVE FEEDBACK®*, www.michaelallosso. com/tsp.html. Accessed 13 June 2023.

Kets de Vries, Manfred F. R.. Reflections on Character and Leadership: On the Couch with Manfred Kets de Vries. Germany, Wiley, 2010.

"Quotes - History Will Be Kind to Me, for I Intend to Write It." *Shmoop*, 11 Nov. 2008, www.shmoop.com/quotes/history-will-be-kind-to-me.html.

Wainwright, Anson. "Mike Tyson: Just How Good Was the Former Undisputed Heavyweight Champion of the World?" *The Ring*, 23 Nov. 2020, www.ringtv.com/613602-mike-tyson-just-how-good-was-the-former-undisputed-heavyweight-champion-of-the-world/.

Made in the USA
Columbia, SC
18 August 2023

21716414R00137